Teams vs. Plunderers

Teams vs. Plunderers

Ed Minnock

Published by Ed Minnock & Associates

Copyright © 2019 by Ed Minnock

Version 2.1

All rights reserved. No part of this book may be reproduced in any form or by any electronic or mechanical means, including information storage and retrieval systems, without written permission from the author, except in the case of a reviewer, who may quote brief passages embodied in critical articles or in a review.

Trademarked names may appear throughout this book. Rather than use a trademark symbol with every occurrence of a trademarked name, names are used in an editorial fashion, with no intention of infringement of the respective owner's trademark.

The information in this book is distributed on an "as is" basis, without warranty. Although every precaution has been taken in the preparation of this work, neither the author nor the publisher shall have any liability to any person or entity with respect to any loss or damage caused or alleged to be caused directly or indirectly by the information contained in this book.

Cover design by Ed Minnock & Associates.

All rights reserved.

ISBN-13: 978-1519696083

ISBN-10: 1519696086

Dedication

For Jody and Killy

Contents

Introduction	1
Chapter 1: Plunderers Lack Internal Moral Principles	6
Chapter 2: Plunderer's Minions: Bad Followers	20
Chapter 3: Plunderer's Rhetoric: Group Lies	32
Chapter 4: Plunderer's Bane: Diversity	51
Chapter 5: Plunderer's Disguise: Wolves in Sheep's Clothing	59
Chapter 6: Plunderer's Revenge	71
Chapter 7: Playing the Game	80
Chapter 8: Overconfidence Trap	87
Chapter 9: An Ethical Team Saves the Day	96
Chapter 10: Building Consensus	118
Chapter 11: Return of the Plunderers	132
Chapter 12: Building Ethical and Effective Organizations	140
Chapter 13: When Tech Companies Attack	154
Acknowledgements	165
Notes and References	166
About the Author	172

Introduction

The technology industry is fertile ground for corporate plunderers. Of course plunderers, or people who enrich themselves at the expense of other people and the environment, can be found in any industry. But the tech industry is particularly fine hunting grounds for these individuals because regulations are rarely able to keep up with the pace of technological advancement, barriers to entry are low, and investors can overvalue companies that appear promising. This combination of factors allows plunderers to make a lot of money in a hurry.

Further, lawmakers, regulators, enforcements agents, and judges don't understand technology—not well enough to write prophylactic laws or regulations or to understand the full repercussions of a plunderer's actions. Consequently, tech plunderers have to do something really brazen, like shipping their customers bricks instead of an actual product, to suffer any serious consequences.

Plunderers' Days are Numbered

Plundering has been enormously profitable for

companies, their short-term investors, and their leaders because it's easier to plunder than to create value for all impacted parties. It's easier to cook the books than make a legitimate profit. It's easier to lay off 1,000 people than to develop successful new products. It's easier to lie about features and benefits than to deliver on promises. It's easier to pollute than to create sustainable operations.

However, the days of easy plundering are numbered. Today, people with morals, particularly young people like millennials, are taking a stand against organizations and individuals that plunder. Social media and the Internet have made it harder for plunderers to hide their transgressions and easier for people with morals to start movements and organize protests and boycotts.

Many companies have learned the hard way that, today, what happens half way around the world doesn't stay there. Walmart was rudely awakened when it learned that up to 14 million Americans won't shop there because of its social and environmental practices.[1]

Ethical Teams

Leaders of many organizations realize that their customer base and workforce are being replaced by young people who care about social and environmental responsibility. So, how can companies find breakthroughs that satisfy all impacted parties: investors, customers, employees, communities, and the

Introduction

environment? The answer: ethical teams.

Ethical teams create value for all impacted parties. They take on audacious goals and search outside of the traditional methods of operation for innovative solutions that satisfy everyone's needs. Ethical teams consider the effects of the organization's decisions on all that may be impacted before taking action—they don't sacrifice morality for the short-term benefit of those in power. Best of all: the results produced by ethical teams are superior, long-lasting, and a lot faster than one would think.

This Book

In his ground-breaking book *The Innovator's Dilemma*, Clayton Christenson states, "If you want to understand why something happens in business, study the disk drive industry" because in this industry, change is "pervasive, rapid, and unrelenting." During a twenty-year period, 129 companies entered the disk drive market and 109 failed.[2] I worked for three of these disk drive companies, as well as two tape drive companies that encountered the same rapid pace of technological development. I also led turnarounds in U.S. scanner and digital camera businesses as technology advanced at breakneck speed and global competition attacked.

This book contains stories of the plunderers I came across during my career in the technology industry, as well as stories about some of the awesome people that I worked with and the ethical dilemmas I and they faced in an industry rife with plunderers. These stories explain how plunderers operate, how they reach the highest levels of management within corporate America, and, most importantly, how companies can incorporate ethical teams and stave off plunderers.

This book is for working professionals that want to build and/or be part of organizations that are both ethical and effective. Here are the steps to build an ethical and effective organization:

1. **Hire ethical and effective leaders.** Ethical and effective leaders will look for solutions that meet everyone's needs and avoid plundering. As like attracts like, ethical and effective leaders will attract, and hire, people that are also ethical and effective.

2. **Weed out plunderers.** Weeding out plunderers can be challenging because they often hold the highest positions in an organization. So, it's essential that up-and-coming plunderers in the ranks are identified and managed out before they do lasting damage.

3. **Build ethical teams.** The key to building an ethical team is (1) staffing it with people with needed skillsets and (2) creating a supportive environment in which the team can operate. One wrong team member can cause a team to break down into defensive, unproductive behavior, and, as a result, accomplish nothing.

Introduction

4. **Build consensus.** Success in the face of adversity requires leaders that possess the ability to build consensus among larger teams made up of people with very different, but complementary, expertise.

Chapter 1

Plunderers Lack Internal Moral Principles

I scanned the Wall Street Journal as the airplane taxied toward the runway. My employer, MiniScribe, just reported its third quarter 1988 earnings: best quarter ever, $15 million in net income.[1]

In the article, chief executive officer (CEO), Chairman, and renowned corporate turn-around expert Q. T. Wiles bragged, "We have achieved the best results in our company's history and now have a three-year track record of consecutive growth in revenues and increasing profitability." The Journal gushed over MiniScribe, the only disk drive company to dodge that year's industry-wide slump. In reality, MiniScribe lost $2.2 million that quarter.[1]

I had joined MiniScribe as an engineer in March 1988. MiniScribe sold disk drives to computer companies for their personal computer products. When applying for the position, friends and colleagues told me it was a good company; business journals touted MiniScribe as a great company, with a great CEO.

Plunderers Lack of Internal Moral Principles

At first, I worked in a cleanroom trying to improve production yield and quality, but after a few months I was asked to work with MiniScribe's component suppliers to improve their product quality. I would soon learn that the biggest problem suppliers had wasn't product quality, but that MiniScribe wasn't paying them.

A colleague and I flew to California to help Solectron, a printed circuit board supplier, improve its product quality. When we arrived, the account manager told us that he wouldn't meet with us until MiniScribe paid its multi-thousand dollar bill. Intent on getting the job done, I called our purchasing manager and asked if MiniScribe could make at least a partial payment on what was owed. The answer: "no." It could have been worse. Some suppliers had refused to ship components to MiniScribe until MiniScribe made at least a partial payment.

Despite MiniScribe's reportedly strong earnings and the CEO's inspiring words, the company appeared to have a cash flow problem. It was time to find a new job. I updated my resume and planned to contact a few companies next week. I also planned to contact the accounting department to obtain a check for months of unreimbursed travel expenses. I could use the money, having just bought a used car.

When I arrived at work the following Monday, my boss asked me to spend the rest of the year in South Korea helping a supplier that makes the all-important head-actuator assembly. I asked what my other options were—he shook his head. Two days later, I was on a plane to South Korea, without an expense reimbursement check.

I arrived in Seoul, spent a night at the Hyatt, and took the early morning bus to Chung Gou, an industrial town sixty miles south of the North Korean border. The head-actuator assembly was made in a clean, modern factory with well-trained and fairly treated workers. Although MiniScribe owed this supplier a lot of money, the team assigned to MiniScribe still worked hard to deliver a quality product on schedule. While visiting, we set up a source inspection process that allowed approved head-actuator assemblies to be routed directly to the MiniScribe cleanroom, which saved on the costs of inspection and rejections.

I soon became familiar with soju, Korea's popular liquor, and kimchi, Korea's fermented vegetables. But in December, my weekly check-in call to MiniScribe went unanswered. The following week, a stranger answered the phone and brusquely informed me that the people I used to talk with were laid off.

When I returned to MiniScribe's Colorado-based headquarters in January, the place was awash in incredible rumors. A cleanroom technician told me that production staff were ordered to pack scrapped parts in boxes as finished goods. That's illegal—I didn't believe him.

It was definitely time to find another job. Meanwhile, my boss wanted me back in South Korea immediately. I was scheduled to leave in two days, but the company now owed me over $5,000 in travel expense reimbursements. Worst case scenario: MiniScribe declares bankruptcy while I'm in South Korea, I get laid off and have to buy my plane ticket back, without ever being reimbursed.

The next day, I called the accounting department and again asked for an expense reimbursement check. I was told I would get a call when the check is ready. Having heard nothing by 4:00 p.m., I drove to the accounting department building and asked for my check. I was told it couldn't be processed that day. I explained that I was scheduled to fly to South Korea tomorrow and would really appreciate a reimbursement check before I left. Again, I was told it couldn't be done. As I wasn't interested in continuing to provide MiniScribe with zero-interest loans, I told the woman in the accounting department that if I didn't get a check, I wouldn't be getting on a plane. Reluctantly, she walked into the office of the chief financial officer (CFO). Five minutes later, I was handed a check. I thanked her and left.

When I returned to my office, my boss was waiting for me. The CFO had called to demand that I be fired. A few years later, the CFO and Q.T. Wiles would go to prison for accounting fraud along with other MiniScribe executives.

In February 1989, I found a new job. Over the next few months, MiniScribe's massive accounting fraud was uncovered—it was triggered by shipping bricks.

Teams vs. Plunderers

Smoking Gun—Bricks!

In 1985, Q.T. Wiles, then a partner in the Hambrecht and Quist venture capital firm, took over as CEO and Chairman of the nearly bankrupt MiniScribe. Wiles was known as "Dr. Fix-it," having been credited with turning around several companies.[2] To "fix" MiniScribe, Wiles reorganized the company into five divisions, and then informed division managers that they had new financial goals to meet. If these goals were met, the division managers could receive bonuses of up to 100 percent of their salary; if the goals were missed, they faced reassignment or termination. MiniScribe's sales and profit margins soared immediately. The company's stock price jumped from $3 to $18, handsomely rewarding Wiles and the other partners at Hambrecht and Quist.[1]

But in September 1987, a physical inventory revealed that actual inventory was $15 million less than what was recorded.[1] This inventory deficit had been building for nearly a year. In January 1987, a $2 million inventory hole was discovered by auditors. To hide the problem, a division manager and a finance manager broke into the trunk of the auditor's car and changed the numbers.[2]

Wiles was unaware of the smaller January inventory discrepancy, but he was well aware of the $15 million deficit. Instead of taking the required $15 million write down, Wiles ordered managers to "gross up" the inventory, meaning fill the hole. To fill the hole,

Plunderers Lack of Internal Moral Principles

MiniScribe's managers developed an elaborate fraud plan, with Wiles' full knowledge and approval.

First, an empty warehouse was rented in Boulder, Colorado. Next, ten 48-foot trailers were procured, along with 26,000 bricks from the Colorado Brick Company. Finally, a computer program called "Cook Book" was written to generate serial numbers for the brick "inventory."[1,2] Beginning on Saturday, December 18, 1987, the 26,000 bricks were loaded onto pallets, shrink wrapped, and boxed at the Boulder warehouse.[2] The size, shape, and weight of each brick pallet was roughly the same as a pallet of disk drives. The brick pallets were then loaded onto trailers.

To fill the remaining inventory gap, obsolete parts were relabeled as current inventory and some inventory was double counted. The $15 million inventory hole was filled. But it was the end of the 1987 fiscal (and calendar) year, and MiniScribe managers were on the verge of missing their financial goals. To keep their jobs and secure their bonuses, finished goods were shipped to third-party warehouses and booked as revenue. Imaginary sales of brick finished goods were also booked as revenue. After the year-end books closed, MiniScribe reversed the "ghost" sales and transferred the brick inventory back into finished goods.[2]

They got away with all of it.

In 1987, MiniScribe reported an annual revenue of $362 million, a whopping 96 percent increase over 1986. The company also reported income before interest and taxes of $36 million, a 49 percent increase.[1] Writing off the $15 million would have reduced 1987 income to $21 million, $3 million below MiniScribe's 1986 income. Instead, 1987 was reported as a great year. Wall Street was impressed.

In February 1988, a month before I joined, Q.T. Wiles took a break from directing what would become one of the most famous frauds in history to share the secrets to his success in an interview with Inc. Magazine. In the article, Wiles was referred to as the "Company Doctor."[3] During the interview, Wiles boasted that he was uniquely qualified to fix companies that other CEOs couldn't due to his ability to break a company down into its smallest components, see the details, and make emotion-free decisions. He prattled on about his thirteen disciplines, including ruthless quarterly "Dash" meetings where managers were grilled on every operational detail. Ethics were not among his tenets.

As the disk drive industry slump persisted, MiniScribe continued to cook the books. MiniScribe's third quarter 1988 net income was exaggerated by $17 million.[1] But at the end of 1988, MiniScribe managers were on the verge of missing their numbers again. To meet these year-end revenue and profit goals, more bricks and scrapped components were packaged, and customers were offered deep discounts if they bought product before the end of the year. Amid layoffs and the ongoing fraud, MiniScribe lost control of its inventory. Bricks were shipped by mistake. By the time the mistake was realized, it was too late to recall the trucks. When the bricks arrived, the customer called the Department of Justice.[1]

Q.T. Wiles and fifteen other company executives were charged with fraud. To convict, prosecutors had to prove that Wiles and others intentionally mislead investors. Otherwise, the defense can win with arguments of risk-taking and mistakes. In a street crime, like a drug bust and theft, there is usually a smoking gun, or clear evidence that a crime has been committed, such as the drugs and stolen merchandise. But in white-collar crimes, "smoking guns" are often harder to find. If they exist at all, they're in the form of obscure emails or documents. Here there was a smoking cannon - thousands of bricks masquerading as functioning, ship-ready disk drives. Prosecutors had to then prove that Wiles was complicit in the fraud. During the trial, Wiles' lawyer argued that Wiles knew nothing of the fraud and had been duped by his underlings.[4] Unfortunately for Wiles, there was overwhelming evidence that he had directed the fraud on a daily basis. And a manager testified that Wiles told him that the government "wouldn't put a seventy-year-old man in jail." The jury didn't buy the "duped" or the "old man" arguments. Wiles was wrong—and he began serving a three-year sentence at age seventy-five.

The jury found that Wiles filed false financial statements with the U.S. Securities and Exchange Commission (SEC), and then used those false statements to secure a $90 million loan from Standard

Charter Bank in early 1988. MiniScribe later defaulted on this loan. The jury also convicted Wiles of insider trading, finding that Wiles sold $1.7 million of MiniScribe stock knowing the company's financial statements were a farce and the company was in a death spiral. For this insider trading, Wiles was fined $1.5 million. He also paid out $9.7 million to settle civil law suits.[1]

MiniScribe's auditor, Coopers & Lybrand, was fined $140 million for failing to detect a rather obvious accounting fraud. Hambrecht and Quist paid a $21.5 million fine. MiniScribe entered bankruptcy and was sold to Maxtor, a competitor, for $46 million. Hundreds of employees lost their jobs. Stockholders lost everything.[4]

First Time Fraud or First Time Caught?

Besides the obvious financial benefit, why would Q.T. Wiles plunder a company and put his gold-plated reputation at risk? It appears that Wiles believed that he would never suffer any serious consequences, even if caught. He said that the government wouldn't put a seventy-year-old man in jail. And if MiniScribe hadn't actually shipped bricks to a customer, he might not have been caught. By the time the FBI arrived at MiniScribe, the fraud had continued for two years. Wiles had gotten away with filling a $15 million dollar inventory shortfall mostly with bricks and packaging scrapped inventory as finished goods. He also got away with shipping disk drives to third party warehouses and booking it as revenue. And he even got away with pretending to ship bricks to customers and booking these ghost shipments as revenue. The magnitude of the fraud perpetuated at MiniScribe begs the question: was MiniScribe the first time Wiles committed fraud, or was it just the first time he was caught.

Plunderers' Apparent Lack of Morals

Q.T. Wiles and many other plunderers are well paid and highly educated. The ranks of plunderers convicted of accounting fraud include three dozen alumni from Harvard.[5] One might expect that these smart, well-paid plunderers to take a rational approach and perform complex analyses, weighing benefits versus risks of adverse consequences before plundering.

Nope. They just plunder. They see an opportunity to make money or seize power, and they take it. And interviews with convicted white collar criminals after their release from jail revealed that most plunder with a clear conscience.[5] They plunder with a clear conscience because, at least in the realm of business, they have no internal morals, no principles of right and wrong. The saying, "listen to your gut" won't help them because they have no internal metric of right and wrong.

When you "listen to your gut," you are checking in with your own personal set of internal moral principles, or the set of beliefs that guide a person's actions. People with internal moral principles believe that all people should be treated justly and fairly; these people strive to act in such a way that is "just" and "fair" to others.[6] Others with internal moral principles go a step further; they believe that all actions should take into account the potential repercussions on future generations, and thus will make decisions that consider the long-term impact on society or the environment. And they still abide by the principles that their religion or social class have instilled in them. Internal moral principles are foundational to movements that support human rights, civil rights, or gender equality. However, studies have shown that the behavior of at least 75 percent of adults, both men and women, is not driven by internal moral principles, such as fairness and justice.[6]

The 75 percent can be broken down into two groups. The first group, less than 10 percent of adults, are plunderers. Their Machiavellian behavior is driven by the possible rewards from their actions, such as money or power, which are external motivators. Plunderers will lie, cheat, and steal to make money and/or gain power, and are unconcerned about the methods used to achieve these gains. If caught, they may apologize. But they're not sorry they plundered. They're sorry they were caught, and they're trying to minimize their punishment.[5]

The second and largest group includes the vast majority of adults. An individual in this group wants to be seen as a good person or good employee. Their behavior is driven by what pleases or is approved of and rewarded by people they consider important, also external motivators. Important people can include

Plunderers Lack of Internal Moral Principles

parents, spouses, friends, teachers, and religious leaders. These people follow rules, laws, and directions unless a more trusted advisor tells them not to. In organizations, people in the second group look to peers, superiors, and celebrated leaders to determine how to behave. If they plunder, people in the second group probably will too, especially if directly pressured by people they consider important.

Only people in the third group, which accounts for less than 25 percent of adults, behave in accordance with internal moral principles. These people will resist plundering even when pressured by peers, superiors, or other people they consider important.[6]

The term "internal principles" can be confusing. Taking moral action prescribed by a religion to obtain afterlife rewards and avoid afterlife punishment doesn't qualify as an internal principle because actions are in response to an external, rather than an internal, motivator. Doing charity work because your company encourages it doesn't count for the same reason. Loyalty is typically considered a positive trait, but it is situational. Loyalty to peers and superiors who plunder enables plundering. G. Gordon Liddy, the planner and commander of the 1972 Watergate break-in, professed absolute loyalty to President Nixon. Liddy refused to cooperate during the Watergate investigations. After serving a 52-month sentence, Liddy claimed that his silence bought Nixon two additional years as president.[7]

Here, an individual's internal principles describe

the reasoning process that determines how one acts. Like the laws of physics, the internal principles repeatedly guide decision making, despite external pressure. The people in this group will refuse money and power if it makes them complicit in actions that harm other people or the environment. These people will raise issues that plunderers and their followers don't want raised. When internal avenues are exhausted, these are the people will blow the whistle.

These three groupings represent a capacity for behavior. People can behave at their group level or below, particularly if they're under pressure. There is no statistically significant difference between men and women.

Because the behavior of the people in group two, that is, the behavior of the vast majority of adults, depends upon the examples that leaders set and the potential reward for their actions, it's important that leaders are ethical and require ethical behavior. In corporate America, that does not appear to be the case.[5]

Although there is a wide variation and some of the data is a bit dated, it appears that on average, the highest levels in Corporate America are staffed by the least ethical people. CFOs are, on average, less ethical than middle management. CEOs and members of boards of directors are, generally, less ethical than CFOs. And accounting partners, including the people who approve company financial statements, have ethics in line with those who peddle Viagra and opioids.[5]

Plunderers Lack of Internal Moral Principles

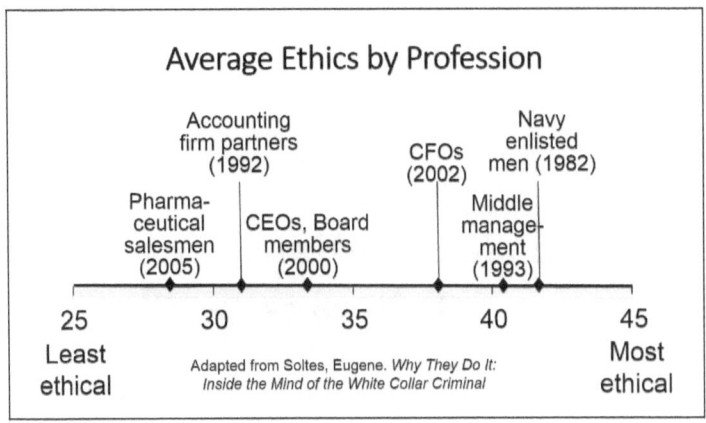

Some argue that media hype creates a false narrative, and that only a small number of CEOs plunder. But leaders don't get into trouble every time they lie, cheat, or steal. They only get into trouble when they're caught. Plunderers are often lionized, as Q.T. Wiles was, right up until the moment they're caught.

In 1999, two of the most successful executive recruiters profiled fifty CEOs, who the authors said exemplified great leadership. Readers were encouraged to learn from and pattern themselves after these great leaders. Six of the fifty were promptly convicted of outrageous white-collar crimes.[5] Were the other forty-four all innocent, or were some plunderers who were smart enough not to get caught?

Bottom line: Plundering is widespread because, at the highest level, Corporate America is staffed by the least ethical people, on average, and the majority of adults will plunder if pressured to do so.

Chapter 2

Plunderer's Minions: Bad Followers

"Something happened last week while you were on vacation," my boss Ken said slowly. He took a deep breath, as if bracing himself for an oncoming storm. "Jonas fired Bob." Jonas was Ken's boss, the vice president of manufacturing at Gigabit, (not the real name).

"What? What for!" I demanded. Bob was my best engineer and a good friend.

"Jonas didn't think Bob was doing his job."

"Jonas doesn't have a clue what Bob does."

"Sorry," Ken said. "I wanted you to hear it from me."

I was steaming. I stomped back to my office, muttering obscenities. Jonas had told me to fire people in my department multiple times. I never did. And he never mentioned firing Bob. I always thought Jonas was just blowing off steam when he ranted about terminating people. Maybe he has been serious. I thought he was vile.

Plunderer's Minions: Bad Followers

I called Bob at home. He answered, meeting my outraged tone and questions about what had happened with a calm tone and measured answers. He said last week was difficult, but he didn't like working at Gigabit anyway. Although we sell a good product, Bob said, the lack of effective teamwork was holding back the company. When I asked what he planned to do for work next, Bob said he had an interview this Friday with a company he used to work for. Bob was handling being fired much better than I was.

After hanging up the phone, I hustled to the 9:00 a.m. production meeting run by Jonas. I sidelined myself from the discussion by sitting in the back of the room, and spent most of the meeting studying his face, trying to determine what kind of person fires someone three management levels below him for no reason—and who could be fired next.

Jonas "managed" manufacturing by deploying a group of loyal followers who were empowered to bully and intimidate. Jonas rewarded this loyalty with large salary increases and stock options. Some members of his inner circle were not smart, but what they lacked in intelligence, they more than made up for in blind loyalty. Jonas viewed everyone outside this inner circle, including me, with scornful distrust.

Jonas made decisions that were aggressive, risky, and sometimes stupid. These decisions often resulted in products needing to be reworked and irate customers. He managed in such a fashion that when his decisions succeeded, he received the credit—but when they failed, as they often did, someone else was set up to take the blame. Often, that someone was me or those that worked in my department.

I managed the department of manufacturing engineering. Despite this, I had no say in important decisions that affected my department's ability to do its job. This lack of input, however, was no excuse for the mistakes and problems that stemmed from Jonas's decisions, regardless of the difficulty of the task at hand or the effort my team and I put into trying to solve these problems. The people in my department worked lots of overtime, but it was never enough.

Like your typical school yard bully, Jonas was thin-skinned. Questioning his decisions caused him to fly into a rage and start shouting at decibels that rivaled those from a death metal concert. I sometimes considered bringing a set of earplugs to meetings in which I suspected I might disagree with one of Jonas's decisions.

One day, Jonas stopped by my office and said, "I don't like company sponsored sports. People get hurt and miss work. I'd rather they die. That way I can replace them." This was his subtle way of telling me not to race on the company's ski team that year. I didn't.

Jonas, who had a quarter million in founders' shares in the company, made sure all the managers knew that he planned to retire early, stay rich, and never have to work again.

After working my usual Saturday shift, I picked up

my girlfriend (soon-to-be wife) for dinner and a movie. Knowing that Bob had been fired, she brought a gift to cheer me up. I chuckled as I unwrapped it—she had given me a copy of *Leadership Secrets of Attila the Hun*. That Sunday, I updated my resume and browsed the *Attila* book. It neatly summed up Attila's management principles: death for the disloyal, lust for leadership, and courage to win at all costs. These barbaric principles aligned perfectly with how I saw Jonas's approach to leadership.[1]

The following week was tougher than usual. On Tuesday, I got into a heated argument with Jonas' lead minion, the production control manager. On Thursday, I lost my cool with another one of Jonas' minions, the production manager. Perhaps hearing about these altercations, Jonas stepped up the pressure. At the end of the daily 9:00 a.m. production meeting, Jonas reviewed the few action items he had assigned, which were usually high-dollar inventory or schedule problems. Previously, my name had been tied to only a couple items per week. Now my name was on a couple items each day.

In that Friday's meeting, I announced that my team had completed two of my assigned items that morning with process change notices. Then I noticed my name was on the last action item too—Jonas had assigned it to me at the end of yesterday's meeting. I had forgotten about it.

I started to sweat as Jonas got closer to my yet-to-be-resolved item. Did I dare admit that I had forgotten something? No way. After Jonas read the last action item, I announced in a measured tone that the second process change notice resolved that action item as well—a bald-faced lie. But no one disputed my claim, and the meeting ended without raised voices. I beelined for the door.

"Ed," said a voice behind me, halting my escape. It was the quality manager who had approved the second process change notice minutes before the morning's meeting. "I have a question about your second process change notice." I led him away from the crowd filing out of the room. He asked how that process change notice addressed the last action. I confessed that it didn't and thanked him for not blowing my cover.

Knowing that I had dodged a bullet, I retreated to my office and slumped down in my chair. Jonas's top minions, the production control manager and the production manager, had also signed the second process change notice right before the meeting. Given their loyalty to Jonas, and the heated exchanges we had had earlier that week, they would have loved to expose my lie. Perhaps they hadn't really read the notice or, perhaps, they weren't paying attention when they had read it. In any event, I suspected that I was climbing to the top of Jonas' list of people he planned to fire.

I thought about how to avoid the proverbial chopping block as I munched on an apple. A devious idea crept into my head. What if Jonas thought I agreed with his medieval management style? Maybe then I'd be included in his inner circle and could have a say in the decisions that affect my department. Maybe then manufacturing would perform better, and my staff would have to spend fewer hours cleaning up Jonas's messes. And maybe my job would be a little more secure and little less miserable as well. These benefits seemed promising, and, at the time, I didn't consider the other ramifications of this decision—that I would be deceiving Jonas. I was facing an ethical dilemma. **An ethical dilemma is when a person must choose between two or more options, all of which are morally valid, and the resulting choice causes one or more morally valid options to be compromised.**

Over the weekend, I purchased a new copy of the *Attila* book. The following week, I left it on Jonas' desk with a note that simply said, "Great read." A few days later, Jonas stopped by my office and exclaimed that it was the best book he had ever read. He had the company purchase twenty copies and demanded his minions read it. He even began quoting the book in staff meetings.

The following week, I was in Ken's office, when in stormed a visibly angry Jonas. Sensing that I would soon be in need of those noise cancelling headphones, I immediately stood and offered to leave. Jonas said I should hear this too. Two weeks ago, he would have ordered me to leave.

Jonas told Ken that he had hired consultants to prepare a proposal to buy and fit up a new manufacturing building ten miles away because the current building didn't have enough capacity for next year's volume. Jonas was fuming because the CFO wouldn't give him the $10 million to go through with the project.

This new building was another terrible idea. My team and I met with the product design engineers, who were housed in an adjoining building, nearly every day. They liked hearing what was happening in manufacturing and helped me and my team solve any problems that arose. Jonas's pet project would put me and my team ten miles away, which would make it more difficult for the two teams to collaborate on these problems.

That weekend, I sketched a layout with production lines running north to south on the company campus rather than the current east to west orientation. A north to south layout would increase production capacity by 50 percent because the building was long and thin from north to south: this meant more production and less wasted aisle space.

On Monday, I showed Ken the layout. He liked it. We both presented it to Jonas. Jonas also liked it. He gave me the go-ahead to prepare a detailed layout. I took the opportunity to rebalance the production lines and identify all the required utilities. This, in addition to my normal management job, was a lot of work.

But, a month later, it was done. Jonas approved the plan, it was implemented, and the efficiencies saved the company $10 million. Having proven myself with this project, I had made it into Jonas' inner circle, and was now part of the decision-making team.

Although being part of the inner circle required regular pandering to Jonas's fragile ego, it had significant benefits for the company. Teamwork improved between my department and departments run by other minions. Instead of being a comedy of errors, manufacturing began performing better, just in time to meet an increased demand in volume for our product. Because we could meet this demand, profits were up, and the company's stock rose from the high teens into the 20s and then the 30s.

Jonas was chuffed. His stock options were now worth millions. He bragged to anyone who would listen that he could walk away from his job any day and never have to work again. I received a 15 percent raise and stock options—a stark contrast to last year's modest raise and no stock options. Thanks Attila.

One day, an engineer who worked for me was shredded by Jonas over a minor disagreement. Mad as a wet hornet, the engineer stomped into my office to complain.

I closed the door. The engineer told me that Jonas had stopped him in the hallway to ask about a project. When the engineer told him that he was working on other, higher priority projects, Jonas told the engineer that all of his projects were a top priority. When the engineer disagreed, Jonas flew into a rage, yelling nonsensically about a burning house with kids in it that are going to die.

Teams vs. Plunderers

I told the engineer that Jonas didn't believe in prioritization. Anyone who disagreed had to listen to the same tired refrain, "You've got three kids and your house is on fire. Which kid do you let die?"

"Really," the engineer said, slumping back into the chair. "Is Jonas that stupid?"

"Jonas is a nut job," I said. "He only cares about himself. We have to pretend to agree with him or he'll consider us disloyal and fire us."

After a while the engineer calmed down. Little did I know that Jonas was in the next office, listening in through the wall. The next day Ken called me into his office and told me that Jonas heard everything I had said yesterday and was livid. The charade was over. I expected to be yelled at or fired or both. Instead, curiously, nothing happened.

A week later, the company secured a large order that required changes to the critical purchased tape mechanism. And the production control manager wanted production to rework the in-house inventory. The rework was technically complex—we had never done anything like it. I countered, proposing that the supplier make subassemblies to the new specification. Ken agreed with my suggestion. Then Jonas sided with the production control manager. Ken caved.

To make this decision even riskier, the production control manager scheduled the order for the upcoming weekend even though the shipment wasn't due for weeks. When I protested, Jonas said that the company needed that revenue now. In other words, Jonas would get to play the hero and take credit for saving the day if the company shipped sooner.

My group scrambled to prepare rework procedures. We worked the entire weekend and oversaw the subassembly rework and final production. The shipment went out Monday. But when the shipment was delivered, the customer performed a rigorous qualification test and found a problem relating to the rework. The shipment was returned, and all future orders were put on hold.

Jonas called me into his office and told me that I was 100 percent to blame for this large and very visible failure, which implied that the CEO and other upper-level executives were also aware that I was to blame. A light bulb went off—this was how Jonas was going to seek his revenge for my disparaging comments about him.

Fortunately, I was better prepared than I had been at MiniScribe. I hadn't recently bought a car or a house. I lived in a small apartment and had enough money saved to cover my expenses for six months without a job. I also had put together a short list of the contact information of hiring managers at several companies. I was able to find a new job in six weeks.

But soon after I left, Jonas's dream came true. He retired rich, and never worked another day in his life.

To be or not to be a Bad Follower?

Plunderers need followers to help them plunder. Some followers don't actively contribute to the plundering,

Teams vs. Plunderers

but enable plundering by merely doing their job, that is, keeping the company running smoothly while the plundering takes place.

Plunderers lure bad followers by offering wealth and power.[2] They threaten those that don't fall in line with demotions or setting them up to take the fall for one of the plunderer's poor decisions. During the brief period when Jonas thought I was loyal, he gave me an excellent raise and stock options and a say in company decisions that would affect my and other departments.

Plunderers retain their bad followers, and discourage those that would thwart them, by making the cost of not following high.[2] Jonas screamed at, belittled, refused to remunerate, and even fired employees that he did not consider loyal.

I became a bad follower when I chose to deceive Jonas and give him the *Atilla* book, and then acted in such a way that made him think I supported his poor decisions and medieval management style. Although the company benefitted, as manufacturing performed better, my deceit did nothing to stop Jonas from abusing the people in my department. I should have known better—abusing subordinates was part of Jonas's management style. I had protected myself from such abuse, benefitted from a large raise and stock options, but had ignored an important ethical responsibility—my responsibility to do what was right.

When faced with the decision of whether or not to deceive Jonas, I faced an ethical dilemma. Like all employees, I had a responsibility to follow direction from my boss, Ken, and my boss' boss, Jonas. But I also had a responsibility to do my job successfully and work to ensure my company succeeded. Yet as a manager, I was responsible for the wellbeing of those that worked for me. Finally I had an ethical responsibility to myself—and, ultimately, I knew that I must do what is right.

So, was deceiving Jonas ethical? For years, I regretted deceiving Jonas, not because he ended up finding out what I really thought about him or because I didn't stick around long enough to benefit much from my raise and stock options. I regretted deceiving Jonas because I don't like to be deceived, and I believe it's wrong to deceive people. Looking back now, I realize that I don't regret deceiving Jonas as much as I regret being a bad follower that helped him succeed.

In the end, Jonas got what he wanted. He retired rich. He was a bad leader and a cruel person. His bad actions did not deserve to be rewarded. Instead of helping him succeed, I should have looked for another job as soon as I had heard Bob was fired. Jonas might still have achieved his dream, but I wouldn't have helped him do it.

Bottom line: It's unethical to support a plunderer.

Chapter 3

Plunderer's Rhetoric: Group Lies

"Congratulations!" John extended his hand. "I'm offering you the position of cartridge process engineering manager." As manager of cartridge operations, John just became my new boss.

There was a knock on the door. The quality department vice president entered with an official-looking document in hand. Gesturing with it, he informed John that 10 percent of our customers' cartridges wouldn't work with the new smaller, cheaper disk drives that began shipping this month.

"I've issued a stop-ship order until there's a production screen in place for cartridges. I'm also recalling cartridges from the field." He handed the stop-ship order to John.

"I'm confused," I said. "If all the cartridges work with the old disk drives, isn't the problem caused by the new disk drives?"

The VP glanced my way. "Cartridges have to work in all drives."

Plunderer's Rhetoric: Group Lies

Looking up from the document, John asked if the recall would be expensive.

"No. There aren't many cartridges in the field because you're behind schedule." Having gotten in that jibe, he left.

John sunk back into his chair.

"Is there anything I can do?" I said.

"Can you start your new job now?"

"Sure."

"Try to get production up and running by tomorrow morning. We can't afford to fall further behind."

Before the ink on the promotion documentation was dry, I assembled a team of volunteers to design and build a screen test. The production control department sold my team thirty of the new drives, and we worked all night to both modify the defective drives and ensure that the screen test would do its job.

During this scramble, I asked the volunteers if they had encountered this problem before. I learned that no one from the cartridge operations team had been involved in the development of the new disk drive, and that they were told the new disk drive would perform exactly the same as the old one. Despite this, cartridge operations was being blamed for the drives' defects, and now we were working all night to put a costly workaround in place, while no one tried to fix the underlying issue.

After a few false starts, the screen test was ready to be implemented in the production line at 5:00 a.m.

Teams vs. Plunderers

Saturday morning. The production line team arrived at 6:00 a.m. After catching a few hours of sleep, I returned to work to check on how the implementation of the screen test was going. Finished goods had been successfully screened—and the production line was turned back on.

On Sunday I again stopped by work for a couple hours. Implementing the screen test had reduced the daily output from 1,500 units to 1,300. Cartridge operations was falling further behind schedule, and the cost of reworking the drives and scrapping defective units had increased, making the cartridges less profitable overall.

On Monday morning, the quality department lifted the stop-ship order, allowing the screened cartridges to be distributed to customers. On Monday afternoon I attended my first production control meeting. When the production control manager ridiculed the cartridge operations department for running behind schedule, I pointed out that the problem was caused by the new disk drives, not by the cartridges. The other managers jumped on me like a football fumbled in the end zone— it wasn't the drives that were the problem! They voraciously refuted my claim, stopping just short of calling me a liar.

Afterwards, I dropped by John's office and asked why cartridge operations was taking the fall for a problem caused by the new disk drives. He said the introduction of the new disk drive was very successful and thousands had been shipped before customers began to complain. Management then decided it would be better to tell customers that the cartridges needed to be replaced rather than admitting that the new disk drive did not perform exactly the same as the old drive after the marketing department advertised an identical performance.

"Many of our customers already have cartridges that work with the old disk drives," I said. "When those cartridges don't work with the new disk drives, they're going to know that we've lied."

"It's a management decision."

"Is anyone trying to find the defect in the new disk drive?"

"Let's focus on getting back on schedule."

Despite this rebuke, John thanked me for working the weekend and told me that he was in the process of ordering new equipment to increase capacity so the production line doesn't have to be run 24 hours a day.

The management team created a group lie. They said the cartridges were to blame for the defect so the company could continue to ship defective disk drives without having to invest time and money to fix the issue.

A few days later, John sent me to Texas to help the company's largest customer, a computer products and disk drive reseller, set up its own screen test so it could turnaround product to its customers faster. When one of my technicians and I arrived in Fort Worth, the reseller's procurement manager informed me that he wanted to return the 2,000 new disk drives and have the company replace them with drives that worked. He knew the new disk drives were the problem and called the CEO of my company to inform him of his decision. After the call, the procurement manager agreed to instead keep the inventory and screen the cartridges—I wondered how large a discount he received.

While I was gone, John presented a multimillion dollar request for new equipment to the top management. When I returned, John told me that his presentation went well. But I soon heard another version of this story—the production control manager told me that John was berated over the "problems" in cartridge operations, and that he did not obtain approval to buy the new equipment.

I moved my office into a conference room across from cartridge production. While I was unpacking, Dick, the disk drive engineering manager, decided to pay me a visit. Dick informed me that my team didn't have the technical skills to solve the problems that cartridge operations was facing. That was strange. Dick was the individual most responsible for the quality of the new disk drives. He, more than anyone, should have been in the hot seat for failing to find the defect in the new disk drives before they were shipped to customers. To retaliate, I asked him why the new smaller disk drive didn't work as well as the old disk drive. He said it did. "Really," I said. "If that's true, then why are we spending so much time and money screening cartridges that all work in the old disk drives?" Not to be outdone, Dick retorted that I didn't know what I was talking about because I didn't have a degree in electrical engineering.

We were being blamed for mistakes by the people who actually made the mistakes. We were also called stupid. It was obvious that Dick had a lot to gain from the group lie.

Over the weekend, I prepared a flowchart of production and timed out every step. Monday morning, I met with my team. I reminded them that the removable cartridges were supposed to deliver the lion's share of company's profit, but that we were falling further behind every day, despite running the production line almost nonstop. I announced that we couldn't wait for new equipment. "Throughput needs to double now. We need to be able to meet the production schedule while working a normal two-shift, five-day week. To accomplish this goal, we need to improve the product quality enough to get rid of the screen test." Then I asked my team what we can do to make this a reality.

One of my engineers said he would love to try to speed up the equipment, but he was already spending seventy hours a week on equipment maintenance. Another engineer suggested that we hire technicians to do the equipment maintenance, which would free up the engineers so that they could redesign the equipment. I liked the idea, and we prepared a plan to submit to management: hire four technicians, two for each shift, to maintain equipment so the engineers can redesign the equipment.

Teams vs. Plunderers

I presented our plan to John, but he disagreed with the idea. Instead, John wanted me to hire more experienced engineers. He said my engineers' inability to solve the current problems proved that they were too inexperienced. He must have talked to Dick.

I argued that my team had the skills needed and that they worked well together—they just needed a few technicians to do the urgent work. We agreed to compromise: I agreed to hire three technicians and one experienced engineer. John obtained approval for me to hire, and within a month, we hired an experienced engineer and three technicians, all of which were engineering students.

The following week, John resigned. Dick and the production control manager both told me that John was fired. So, cartridge operations and I had a new boss, Troy, who had previously managed media qualification. John was a nice guy, an ethical guy. But he was not an effective manager. Under his leadership, cartridge operations had not met its financial goals and the product did not satisfy customers. Troy was ambitious, results-oriented, and did not like excuses—a lesson I soon learned when I told him cartridge operations was being blamed for a disk drive problem. It seems he was also in on the group lie.

With four new people on board, we made quick progress. Two weeks later, throughput was 20 percent faster; after a month, it was 50 percent faster. After two months, it had more than doubled. Product quality improved enough that we could drop the screen test.

Plunderer's Rhetoric: Group Lies

Production was now churning out 3,000 cartridges a day, with good quality and a minimum of overtime. Profit increased, and new equipment wasn't needed.

With the screen test gone, we implemented a rigorous audit. Every day, one of my second shift technicians tested thirty just-built disk drives with thirty just-built cartridges in read-write and interchange tests. The audit was designed to catch quality problems and provide information and transparency to counter any more group lies.

My team continued to improve throughput. Soon, production was averaging 4,000 cartridges each day, and the backlog quickly disappeared. Then one of my "inexperienced" engineers found the design flaw in the new disk drives: the wrong resister was implemented in the clock circuit. He informed Dick, and the problem was fixed quickly and quietly. I was ecstatic to be out from under the weight of that burden. I sought out Troy to tell him the good news and found him laughing with another manager in the hallway. When I told him how we had resolved the disk drive problem, his face turned serious. "Don't make a big deal of this." Apparently, Troy wanted the group lie to live on. However, that wasn't going to happen. I did my best impersonation of Paul Revere, and told anyone and everyone who would listen. Troy was not pleased.

A month later, we had the first cartridge failures in the audit test. Twenty percent of the cartridge-drive combinations failed the interchange test but had all passed the write-read test. I quarantined the 4,000 cartridges from the day's production. My engineers quickly figured out that the failures were due to a bad batch of media parts from a new lower-cost supplier that Troy's media qualification group had just introduced into production. I instructed the production line to use a different batch of media, and one of my engineers developed a process to swap out the bad parts.

When I told Troy about this issue, I was sure he would agree with my decision to rework the quarantined cartridges and be pleased that we prevented defective cartridges from reaching customers. Nope. Troy wanted to ship the quarantined cartridges. I was dumbfounded. Had he forgotten about the previous quality problems? Because we disagreed, he told me to test a larger sample. That night my technicians tested 100 cartridges from the quarantined production. The interchange failure rate was the same: 20 percent. I showed Troy the data, but he still wanted to ship the quarantined cartridges. He said customers rarely write a cartridge in one disk drive and read it in another. I reminded him that the sales force promoted interchangeability as a key feature and often demonstrated it in sales calls. Troy scheduled a meeting for the afternoon for us to review the data in detail.

It occurred to me that Troy would gladly ship defective cartridges to avoid having to take responsibility for causing rework, even though the cost was minimal. He was trying to start another group lie—he wanted everyone to think his new supplier was performing perfectly.

Our afternoon meeting was over in one minute. As soon as I arrived at his office, Troy told me to rework the cartridges. He was not happy. I instructed the production line to begin the rework and returned to my office to find a quality engineer waiting for me. She asked what we were going to do with the quarantined cartridges. I told her we were reworking them.

"Really," she said. "I heard you were going to ship them."

"No. We're reworking them right now."

She cleared her throat and shifted uncomfortably. "Maybe I jumped the gun. I told my boss that you were going to ship them."

"You mean the quality vice president?"

"Yes."

From that day on, Troy avoided me like the plague. To this day, I don't know why. Maybe the vice president of quality called him, pressured him into reworking the cartridges, and Troy thought I informed the quality department, which I didn't do. Or perhaps Troy thought I should have asked him before quarantining the cartridges, although he never said as much. Once finished goods are quarantined, word spreads pretty quickly. Regardless, as manufacturing engineering manager, customer satisfaction was my responsibility.

Just as production reached 4,000 cartridges per day,

our competitors introduced new, cheaper products. Sales dropped; so did profit margins and the stock price. Our past quality problems had motivated customers to switch to competitors' products.

During the December managers meeting, Dick raised his hand and asserted that the company needed a round of layoffs to clear out all the "dead wood." I couldn't imagine anyone taking Dick seriously this close to the holidays. But on the Monday before Christmas, at 7:20 a.m., the assistant to a director I hardly knew called and told me to report to the director's office immediately. When I arrived, the director informed me that I had a new job and would be working for him. Apparently I had been on the layoff list until 7:00 a.m., when he decided to hire me. My new job was managing a group responsible for designing, building, and maintaining test equipment for disk drive operations department. It was a demotion, but at least I still had a job.

Troy promoted one of his media engineers into my old job. The company laid off 20 percent of its workforce. Troy had fired me and came close to forcing me out of the company, even though I led a team that tripled throughout, improved quality, and found the design bug in the new disk drives.

Group Lies and the No Harm Principle
The No Harm Principle states that persons involved in or affected by the lifecycle of a product or service should not be harmed. It further stipulates that overall

Plunderer's Rhetoric: Group Lies

harm, including harm to the environment, should be minimized.[1] Business actions are unethical when decision makers take actions that they know or could know cause harm and they have the power to cause the harm or avoid causing the harm. Of course, leaders that cause harm don't broadcast their culpability for the harm they cause. To the contrary, they often create group lies that exonerate them.

The motivation behind group lies is simple—people lie because they think they can (1) get away with lying and (2) benefit from the falsehood. Once a group lie is embedded in a company's rhetoric, those that perpetuate it can harm others with a clear conscience. And the vast majority of employees, the group two employees, will follow along, in order to be seen as good employees and to also benefit from the group lie.

Managers at this company didn't tell customers the truth – "We are continuing to ship defective disk drives because it's cheaper than fixing them." Instead, managers created the group lie that cartridges were to blame and knowingly continued to sell customers defective product. Blaming the problem on the cartridges, rather than fixing the problem in the disk drive, wasted company resources—both in hard supplies, in the number of cartridges that had to be scrapped or reworked, and in man-hours, as the employees in cartridge operation were forced to work needless overtime to implement a screen test. At least one person, John, lost his job in part due to this group lie. And, arguably, the layoffs may not have occurred had customers, dissatisfied with the defective product, not been motivated to switch to competitors' products.

The actions of the managers who made the decision to blame cartridges and deceive customers were unethical, based upon the No Harm Principle. They knew their actions caused harm and had the power to avoid doing harm. From a business perspective, harming customers is foolish—it is literally biting the hand that feeds you. When customers, fed up with the poor quality, ultimately shopped elsewhere, stockholders were also harmed. These managers could have avoided, or at least minimized, the harm caused by and cost incurred due to the disk drive defect by simply fixing the new disk drive.

What struck me as odd was that none of the people who were in on the group lie suffered any negative consequences. In fact, their careers advanced. Troy was promoted, and Dick, the individual most responsible for allowing defective disk drives to ship to customers, was securely employed. By refusing to join in the group lie, I made enemies. After refusing to help Troy create the group lie that his new supplier was performing perfectly, I was demoted and almost forced out of the company.

Masters of Group Lies

The concept of group lies may sound familiar. It's similar to propaganda, which has, time and time again, produced dire consequences. Below are just a few examples of widespread group lies and the destruction

Plunderer's Rhetoric: Group Lies

wrought by them.

In 2017, 72,000 Americans died from opioid overdoses, and millions more were addicted to these painkillers.[2] Many addicts switched to illegal and more deadly drugs like fentanyl and heroin. Addiction destroys a person's life, causing people to lose their jobs, destroying relationships with family and friends, and if a person is caught with illegal drugs, it can result in incarceration. Pharmaceutical companies that produce opioids, like Purdue Pharma, among others, have been careful to avoid publicizing the harm they have caused.

Until the 1990s, opioids were almost exclusively prescribed in hospitals to treat acute cancer and end-of-life pain because educated medical professionals knew that opioids were addictive. But the hospital prescription market was relatively small. Pharmaceutical companies that produce opioids found a way to increase opioid sales: they created the group lie that opioids are not addictive.

In 1995, the Food and Drug Administration (F.D.A) approved Purdue Pharma's OxyContin for use in treating moderate to severe pain. Purdue had conducted no clinical studies on how addictive or prone to abuse the drug might be. Nevertheless, the F.D.A., in an unusual step, approved a package insert for OxyContin stating that the drug was safer than rival painkillers, because of its patented delayed-absorption mechanism. Addicts quickly discovered that

Teams vs. Plunderers

OxyContin could be ground up for snorting and smoking and liquefied for intravenous injection, which produced instant total absorption. Instant total absorption can cause overdoses that depress the respiratory system and result in loss of consciousness and death. The F.D.A. examiner who oversaw the OxyContin evaluation left the agency shortly afterward and joined Purdue Pharma.[3]

Purdue Pharma launched OxyContin with one of the biggest pharmaceutical marketing campaigns in history. Over a 1,000 salesmen were hired. Purdue paid famous doctors to write, talk, and record videos about the virtues of OxyContin, and most important, claim that it is not addictive. Doctors were even offered all-expenses-paid trips to pain-management seminars in places like Boca Raton.[3]

Once this group lie was firmly entrenched, doctors began prescribing OxyContin and other opioids for moderate pain like sprained ankles and toothaches.[3] Each year, American doctors write 250 million opioid prescriptions, which works out to be roughly one prescription for every adult in the U.S.[2] While patients have suffered, the pharmaceutical company executives and owners peddling the opioids have struck it rich. The Sacklers, the family that owns and runs Purdue Pharma, a private company, have amassed an empire worth $13 billion. While vigilantly avoiding connections to Purdue Pharma, the Sacklers have made generous philanthropic donations that have earned prominence in leading museums: the Sackler Gallery in

Plunderer's Rhetoric: Group Lies

Washington, the Sackler Museum at Harvard, the Sackler Center for Arts Education at the Guggenheim, the Sackler Wing at the Louvre, and the Sackler institutes and facilities at Columbia, Oxford, and a dozen other universities.[3]

The Sacklers and other opioid executives are modern-day American drug lords. Although Purdue has been served with over 1,000 lawsuits, the company has thus far managed to get cases thrown out or settled out of court, thanks to aggressive legal defense tactics from some of America's most famous lawyers, including former N.Y.C. mayor Rudy Giuliana.[3]

The Sacklers, other opioid CEOs and executives, and doctors have violated the No Harm Principle; they knew or could have known that opioids are addicting and they had the power to avoid doing harm.

The annual number of deaths and injuries caused by gun violence in the U.S. is staggering. In 2016, guns caused 38,000 deaths and wounded 80,000 people. And it isn't just adults that are being harmed, children account for 5,790 of the total shootings.[4] In 2018, school shootings have occurred nearly every week and policemen have been shot nearly every day. Yet America is the only developed country in the world with these out-of-control levels of gun violence. America is also the only developed country in the world without common-sense gun control laws.

The National Rifle Association (NRA) has arguably been the most effective lobbyist in America. And the

Teams vs. Plunderers

NRA's agenda was simple: make it very easy for anyone to purchase any kind of gun, even semi-automatic rifles. But the NRA hasn't taken credit for America's gun violence. Instead, the NRA has used catchy slogans like "the only way to stop a bad guy with a gun is with a good guy with a gun" to support the group lie that the more people that have guns, the safer society is.

Lawmakers under pressure to meet political party contribution requirements have been seduced into accepting NRA funding and endorsements in exchange for promoting the NRA's agenda.

Because it doesn't have the power to create laws, the NRA has played a minor role in violating the No Harm Principle, despite its effectiveness as a lobbyist. However, lawmakers have blatantly violated the No Harm Principle—they have used their power as leaders to make it easy for dangerous people to obtain dangerous weapons. This is wrong—they knew or certainly could have known, as anyone with common sense knows, that dangerous weapons should be kept away from dangerous people. Imagine the carnage that could result if it was easy for anyone to obtain biological, chemical, or nuclear weapons.

For years, the outrage over mass shootings would blow over a few days after the politicians in the NRA's pockets offered "thoughts and prayers". Then seventeen students and teachers were tragically gunned down with a semi-automatic rifle in Parkland, Florida. This time the outrage didn't blow over. Teenagers across the country took a stand. It began with student survivors courageously speaking out against the lies and hypocrisy of the NRA and its paid-for support from lawmakers. The #NeverAgain and #BoycottNRA movements were born. Within a week, car rental companies, hotels, airlines, and banks, among others cancelled the special offers and discounts they offered NRA members. Now there is an entire generation of young people who have endured lockdown drills and senseless tragedies. They want action, and they know how to use the Internet and social media to get it.

School children know that humans have altered the earth's atmosphere, mainly by burning fossil fuels. As a result the percentage of CO_2 in the atmosphere has increased 35 percent since pre-industrial times, and half of the increase is since 1970. A higher concentration of CO_2 traps heat that would otherwise escape into space, producing a warmer climate.[5]

Yet for decades highly educated and well-paid fossil fuel company CEOs have maintained the group lie that climate science is flawed, even though scientists at these same companies have known since the 1960s that global warming is real and CO_2 from burning fossil fuels is the main cause.[6] The group lie has given fossil fuel companies license to plunder the environment and accelerate climate change, with a clear conscience, as this quote from Greg Boyce, Peabody Energy CEO, shows, "The greatest global danger is not a future environmental crisis predicted by computer models" but the "human crisis of 3.6 billion people who lack easy access to electricity."[7] The solution, according to Boyce, was more coal, which he said was "the only sustainable fuel with the scale to meet the primary energy needs of the world's rising populations."[6] Customers weren't fooled. In 2016, Peabody filed for bankruptcy.

The fossil fuel company CEOs that maintained the group lie that climate science is flawed violated the No Harm Principle. They knew or could have known that their actions caused undue harm to the environment and they had the power to minimize harm.

Fortunately, some companies are listening to customers. Royal Dutch Shell's top management identified a new threat, not peak oil, the sixty-year-old prediction that the global supply of oil would reach a peak and then decline, but peak demand, the prediction that demand for oil will peak within a decade and then decline, as it's replaced by renewable energy.[5] Shell has scrambled to unload billions of dollars of oil projects, including the expensive and dirty oil sands in Canada. Instead, Shell is investing in renewable energy and the infrastructure to deliver it.[8]

Bottom line: Group lies enable plunderers to continue harming others and the environment.

Chapter 4

Plunderer's Bane: Diversity

It was my first day at a new job, and I found myself smack in the middle of a testosterone brawl. The meeting had begun amicably enough, but then the discussion turned to an issue with a supplier that was unable to meet a mechanical part's required tolerance levels. The supplier quality engineer said the tolerance levels were unnecessarily strict and should be loosened. A product design engineering manager retorted that the strict tolerance levels were necessary.

The supplier quality engineer said, "Show me the data."

The product design engineering manager insisted that the engineering department sets the tolerances because it alone understands how the product works.

The supplier quality engineer repeated, "Show me the data."

"You wouldn't understand it."

Before long, they were outright insulting each other, using colorful metaphors to personally disparage one another. I doubted either had the data to back up their assertions about personal hygiene. As the new guy, I wondered how a discussion about mechanical tolerances could turn so nasty so quickly.

After the meeting, I spoke with both of them individually. Turns out they had a troubled working relationship, having worked together on the last few new products, all of which had severe quality problems.

As I met more people, I learned that there were two camps in this company: engineering and manufacturing. Nearly everyone in each camp subscribed to the group lie that the other camp was 100 percent to blame for the company's problems. The more vocal people applied pressure on other camp members to suspend their individual judgement and conform to the narrative that the other camp was totally at fault. Even the vice presidents bashed each other.

People were stereotyped based upon the group that they were working in. The manufacturing folks decided that the people working in engineering were arrogant and incompetent. And the engineering employees decided that the people working in manufacturing were idiots.

This was in-group bias. **In-group bias is forming favorable judgements of and giving preferential treatment to people who are included in your group.** Consequently, in-group bias also causes people to view people in other groups more negatively and treat them worse than you would someone in your group.[1]

Nearly every company has some level of in-group

bias. But the animosity between the groups at this company took the cake. Both groups hoarded information and blamed others regularly for problems. Something else was odd about this company—out of 120 engineers between product engineering and manufacturing engineering, there were only two women and no minorities. There wasn't even a women's bathroom in the product engineering department. A symptom of in-group bias is hiring people who are similar to those already in the group. Here, the company was rife with immature white guys. So when my boss told me that I could hire someone, I knew I needed someone who, in addition to being a good engineer, would be able to wrangle a bunch of adolescent boys. Having worked in the technology industry for years, I knew there was a pool of very capable, very underemployed women. I hired Chris and made sure the woman knew what she was getting into. Chris had the rare ability to get along with people who couldn't get along with each other and used this ability to bridge divides and broker agreements.

A few weeks later, Eve, the only woman in the engineering department, stopped by my office for some advice. Eve had been with the company for less than two years, and it had been her first job out of college. She told me that being the only woman in the engineering department was not fun—she was given the worst assignments, was the last to hear about decisions that impacted her work and was ridiculed for being incompetent if she made a mistake. If one of her white, male, colleagues made a mistake, it was considered an accident and brushed aside. I told Eve that her colleagues failed to realize that the engineering department needed her a whole lot more than she needed them.

Another symptom of in-group bias is rampant stereotyping. Eve's colleagues assumed she wasn't qualified because she was a woman and used any mistakes she made to bolster their belief that she wasn't qualified. This is also known as confirmation bias. **Confirmation bias is interpreting new evidence as confirmation of one's existing beliefs.**

A week later Eve stopped by my office again. She wanted to join my group, and the human resources department had agreed to the transfer—perhaps because Eve gave HR an earful about her experiences working in the engineering department. Now all three women engineers in the building worked for me.

Arthur, the vice president of engineering, was now in hot water for creating a work environment that discouraged diversity. But Arthur didn't think he was discriminating against anyone—he actually believed he was hiring the best engineers, who by sheer coincidence happened to be remarkably similar to him. Armed with this belief, Arthur and his managers felt entitled to mistreat any woman or minority who crossed their path. However, the women and minorities he discriminated against were fully aware.[1] And thanks to Eve, so was human resources (HR). HR tried to persuade Arthur to recruit diverse candidates, but

Plunderer's Bane: Diversity

Arthur refused, maintaining that the engineering department was a meritocracy, and saying that he didn't want to lower the bar.

But Arthur had other problems; his star was falling. Years earlier, he led the development of the company's first product, which was a smash hit. Then competitors attacked and engineering's most recent new products failed to generate the desired revenue or profit. Moreover, the company was now a bigger, more complex organization. The manufacturing and marketing people expected Arthur's engineering department to improve current products and make customized changes for important customers. Arthur resisted. He wanted to develop new products, without interference, just as he did when the company was a startup. As a result, his relationships with other vice presidents soured, which meant that no one rushed to his defense when it came time to consider replacing him, and after a few months, Arthur was replaced by another white guy.

Meanwhile, Chris became Eve's mentor. Together, they set up a performance and reliability testing mechanism that provided the engineering department with statistically reliable, over-night test results on their product designs. Now engineering was fixing problems before products were released to production, rather than after. Product quality improved.

Although product hardware quality was better, the new products were still hard to use and didn't appeal to a wide consumer base. One of the downsides of insular organizations is the inability to relate to diverse customers. So, I started looking for another job. I soon had an offer but faced an ethical dilemma: I felt responsible for the women who worked for me and doubted that other managers would give them a chance.

Having learned my lesson about trying to change the habits of an entrenched leadership team to protect my employees while working for Jonas, I decided to cut and run rather than become a bad follower again. I accepted the offer.

In-Group Bias Doesn't Fit Today's Diverse World

As social creatures, we all seek out groups, which can provide social identity, strength, security, and a sense of belonging in the social world. Groups can be large or small; formal organization or informal gatherings. Examples include family, neighborhoods, states, countries, religions, schools, sports teams, political parties, fraternities, sororities, industries, companies, and departments within companies.[1] Groups can also be an important source of pride and self-esteem, but when people subscribe to in-group bias, and inflate their own worth by disparaging the status and abilities of people that are not in their group, it leads to stereotyping of and discrimination toward those that are not in their group.[1]

Once group members believe they are superior, as in they believe they are smarter, more "American," or more "normal" than people that do not belong in their

Plunderer's Bane: Diversity

group, they may also believe they have license to act against those people. Throughout history, in-group bias has been used to justify discrimination against others. In more extreme examples, it has been used to deprive people not only of employment opportunities, but of civil liberties, freedom, and their lives. In-group bias has been used to justify war and genocide.[1]

Two alarming aspects of in-group bias are (1) how easily it's triggered, and (2) how unaware people are that they're doing anything wrong.[1] The people being harmed are fully aware of the injustice of the discrimination.

Arthur knew that he was hiring engineers who were very much like him. But he rejected the notion that, by doing so, he was discriminating against women and minorities. Instead, he adopted the group lie that white guys make the best engineers, giving his white male managers a feeling of superiority and a license to discriminate. Arthur's inability or unwillingness to collaborate with others set the precedent that effective teamwork with other departments wasn't required, and the company suffered because of it.

The facts are in—increased gender and ethnic diversity in employees correlates with increased profits.[2] A diverse workforce is better able to relate to an increasingly global marketplace. Diversity of ideas and experiences may also result in a team's increased ability to brainstorm outside-the-box ideas, which is an important asset in today's ultra-competitive markets.

Teams vs. Plunderers

Business opportunities have taken me to ten Asian countries, three European countries, the UK, two Scandinavian countries, Israel, and countless trips to Canada and Mexico—this amount of travel is normal across many industries. For a business to achieve its potential, everyone must be treated as a partner, with valid ideas and concerns, regardless of gender, race, religion, or ethnicity. Companies can't afford to keep on employees, particularly leaders, who think they're superior and don't work effectively across departments, geographies, and cultures. And finally, as a practical matter, today's younger workers don't want to work at companies with old boys' club rules and discrimination.

Bottom Line: Discrimination reduces diversity in employees; without a diverse employee pool, companies suffer. As leaders are responsible for the success of the company, those that do not stop discrimination are not doing their job.

Chapter 5

Plunderer's Disguise: Wolves in Sheep's Clothing

"This year we will no longer be a one-product company," announced Richard, the CEO, in a January all-hands meeting. "This year we will ship three new products: a new, higher capacity tape drive and two tape libraries." He smiled paternally "I'd like to thank all of you for your hard work. It's because of your efforts that this company is a success."

Richard was well-liked. He was warm, friendly, polite, articulate, impeccably dressed, and a consummate professional. He held company-wide meetings four times a year, and always made sure to thank everyone during these events. Richard emphasized that all employees were in this together, and to prove it, every employee received stock options when hired.

When Richard finished his remarks, Hank, the senior vice president of operations, stood to add that the hiring freeze would be lifted briefly to hire a few people to work on the new tape libraries. There was a stark contrast between the two men—Hank was not well liked. He was rude, crude, unprofessional, and often looked like he slept in his clothes. He was quick to anger, didn't hesitate to fire people, and kept the engineering, manufacturing, and quality departments consistently understaffed.

The new strategy was an aggressive one, given that the startup, which had required four years, tons of overtime, and sheer luck to develop one successful product, now planned to develop, build, and ship three new products at the same time on accelerated schedules.

As the manager of the manufacturing engineering department, I was responsible for the quality and cost of the shipped product. My boss's boss, the manufacturing vice president, made his expectations clear by stating firmly, "No half-baked products on the production line." He was particularly worried about the new tape libraries; the company had never made any before.

Several prototypes of the new tape drive had already been built, and the production process was nearly ready to go. Data reliability on the new device was pretty good, although not as good as it was on the original tape drive, given that the increase in capacity was accomplished by cramming twice as much data onto the tape, resulting in a lower signal to noise ratio and, accordingly, an increased likelihood of

Plunderer's Disguise: Wolves in Sheep's Clothing

interference garbling the data.

But design of the tape libraries hadn't begun. To lead the design of the tape libraries, the engineering vice president hired Rock, a very experienced engineering manager. Rock, in turn, quickly staffed his team by hiring a few engineers. To develop the production processes for the tape libraries, I hired an engineer and technician as well.

Soon after Rock was hired, the quality manager and I met with him to discuss how we were going to work together. I told Rock that, given the accelerated schedule required here, clear lines of communication between the engineering, manufacturing, and quality departments was essential. Rock said there was no time for that, and insisted that his team, located in another building, be left alone. When I objected, he said he knew all about manufacturing and reliability, and that he would take care of it. I was stunned. The tape drive design engineers had always worked with my team before, and it was a terrible idea to not work out potential production issues as the product's design evolves.

Four months later, Rock presented his concept designs to my team and the quality group. From a manufacturability and reliability perspective, Rock's concept designs were so bad that I told him to go back to the drawing board.

"We must move forward, or the end-of-year schedule will be missed," Rock said. "And missing this deadline is not an option." Although Rock had said that he was committed to manufacturability and reliability, his actions indicated that he was only concerned with meeting the deadline.

During the summer, Rock's group finished the detailed design of the tape libraries and built a few engineering prototypes, with tender loving care. Meanwhile, with engineering's help, my team built more production prototypes of the new tape drive. Several were sent to large customers that had bought the first tape drive to see what they thought. The customers were not impressed. They said they wouldn't purchase the new tape drive unless the data reliability improved. This didn't mean much—the same customers had said as much about the old tape drive product as well, and then ended up buying it anyway.

In early fall, my team tried to build tape library prototypes with Rock's help. It was a disaster. Significant product and process design changes had to be made, resulting in both teams putting in significant overtime, yet production yield and product reliability remained terrible. When the problems weren't resolved by late November, I stopped by Rock's office to inform him that we would not be able ship the tape libraries to customers on schedule. After a pained discussion, Rock agreed. He and I told our respective managers that fundamental design changes had to be made and that the tape libraries would not ship this year. The manufacturing vice president was pleased to hear this.

Three days later, Hank sent an email to everyone announcing that the engineering, manufacturing, and

Plunderer's Disguise: Wolves in Sheep's Clothing

quality departments would work every day in December except Christmas day. On the bottom of the email he wrote in capital letters, "MAKE NO MISTAKE. ALL THREE NEW PRODUCTS WILL SHIP THIS YEAR."

Hank seemingly loved making employees work overtime. Two years ago, he ordered mandatory 54-hour work weeks until the data reliability improved enough on the first product that IBM would purchase it. After three months, and no data reliability improvement, Hank fired the vice president of engineering. IBM ended up buying the product anyway. The mandatory 54-hour weeks were particularly tough on single parents, and several people resigned.

Here we go again.

Hank called a meeting with all the managers. He sat at the head of the table with the vice presidents of engineering and manufacturing on either side. Hank told us that our jobs were on the line, and that only a doctor's note would exempt employees from the mandatory overtime. I wondered internally whether Hank knew that the tape libraries didn't work. When Hank opened the meeting up for questions, I decided that someone had to let him know, and announced that, while the new tape drive worked fairly well, both tape libraries were disasters waiting to happen, and it would be a mistake to ship them to customers. I had struck a nerve. Hank practically shouted at me, saying that my @#$%^&* job was to develop the production processes that build quality products, not to second-guess management's decisions. He reiterated that all three products would ship by year's end, then stared me down from across the table, as if daring me to contradict him again.

The threat of being fired, and Hank's prolonged eye contact, made me tense. To calm down, I started leaning back in my chair, further and further. Just as Hank looked away to tell the manufacturing vice president to get his people in line, my chair went over backward. Instinctively, I kicked up my right leg, and the edge of my shoe caught the underside of the table just before my head hit the floor. There I was—frozen—with my head hovering a foot above the floor and my right foot precariously wedged under the table. I strained to pull myself up but couldn't quite manage it. The seconds ticked by, and it felt like I had been in this predicament for an eternity. I took a deep breath, heaved with all my might, and managed to right my chair. Luckily, the executives were talking among themselves and didn't see my chair go over backward, but the rest of the managers burst out laughing.

December was a blur: build, test, rework. A less cheerful Richard dropped by Production. He asked if we were working every day except Christmas. I told him that we were. He responded that he should have ordered mandatory overtime sooner. I then realized that Richard, not Hank, had ordered the mandatory overtime and had made the decision to ship the tape libraries. I'll bet it had been Richard ordering overtime all along, having Hank play the bad guy so Richard could continue to pretend to be a warm and fuzzy CEO. Before the end of the month, we shipped the new products. By the year's end, all three new products had rung up respectable sales, making the fourth quarter a huge financial success for the company, and resulting in a jump in its stock price.

In January, absenteeism spiked as employees, exhausted from the mandatory overtime, fell ill. More bad news came our way: several major customers told us that their decision not to use the new tape drive was final. Then came the really bad news: both tape libraries were recalled due to unacceptable reliability. The stock price plummeted, and Rock was fired immediately. Richard, Hank, and the engineering vice president were furious with Rock for deciding in late November that the tape libraries were not ready to be shipped by the end of the year, especially after he had maintained for months that they would be ready. Hank stopped by my office to tell me that he and Richard were very disappointed with my inability to build tape libraries with acceptable reliability.

Plunder, then Kill the Messengers

The decision to develop, build, and ship three products at once on accelerated schedules was disastrous: None of the products met their financial goals, so investors lost money. Employees were burned out and many became sick. Customers received and returned defective products, damaging the company's reputation.

When Richard ignored the fact that the tape libraries didn't work and ordered mandatory overtime to get the products out the door, he assured the failure of these products. But, instead of taking responsibility for this failure, Richard and Hank blamed the people who told them the products didn't work. Rock took the biggest hit, having lost his job. I was blamed too, although I kept my job. From this experience, I learned that Richard wasn't the warm and friendly CEO he pretended to be. He was a wolf in sheep's clothing, a plunderer who exploited the workforce for his own gain. I'll never know what led Richard to think this little startup could develop, build, and ship three products at once on accelerated schedules. My guess is he didn't give it much thought at all.

Wolves

In 2000, Vice President Sharron Watkins jumped over her boss, CFO Andy Fastow, to inform Enron CEO and Chairman Ken Lay of the massive accounting fraud she had uncovered. Watkins thought Lay was a man of integrity, and that he would put a stop to it.[1] But Lay wasn't going to stop it. He was the architect and had directed Enron's plundering since the 1980s. Lay did not appreciate Watkins' disclosure and immediately asked Enron's lawyers if Watkins was protected by any whistleblower laws. She was not. (At the time, employees of publicly traded companies were not protected against retaliation by whistleblower laws.

Plunderer's Disguise: Wolves in Sheep's Clothing

They are now.) Watkins could have been fired.[2]

Ken Lay held himself out to be a self-made man, a captain of industry, and a man of integrity. He was Houston's hero, having donated millions to worthy charitable causes. As Enron's CEO and Chairman, he often waxed poetic about Enron's values. But behind this facade, Lay was a plunderer who made a fortune defrauding stockholders.[1]

For years, Citigroup's vice president of risk management, Richard Bowen, tried to stop Citigroup's practice of buying high-risk home mortgages, packaging them as AAA (the highest rating) mortgage bonds, and selling them to unwitting customers.[3] But he never contacted the right people.

In 2007, after billions of dollars of AAA junk had been sold, Bowen finally wrote an email to Citigroup's top management, which included the then Chairman of the Board and former U.S. Treasury Secretary Robert Rubin. Bowen's email blankly asserted that Citigroup had violated the Sarbanes-Oxley Act and that the bank was at risk of incurring huge losses.[2] Bowen thought that a letter to Rubin would put an end to Citigroup's plundering. Bowen couldn't have been more wrong. Not only was he ignored, he was stripped all responsibilities and put on administrative leave.[3]

Bowen contacted the Occupational Safety and Health Administration, claiming Citigroup had retaliated against him, but his complaint was settled with a severance check.[3] Next, Bowen decided to blow the whistle on Citigroup. In July 2008, two months before the financial crisis, Bowen approached the Securities and Exchange Commission (SEC), testified against Citigroup, and provided the agency with 1,000 pages of documents that he believed clearly proved that Citigroup's top management, including Robert Rubin, broke the law. Not only did the SEC fail to act on this evidence, but it also buried Bowen's testimony. The SEC denied numerous requests for access to Bowen's file under the Freedom of Information Act. As support for these denials, the SEC claimed that the material was "confidential" and included Citigroup "trade secrets."[3]

In May 2009, after Citigroup and other banks had been bailed out, Congress created the ten-member Financial Crisis Inquiry Commission (FCIC).[2] Bowen testified before the FCIC, implicating Rubin. The FCIC then hauled Rubin in to tell his side of the story. Afterwards, the FCIC recommended that Rubin be investigated by the Department of Justice (DOJ). But DOJ declined, and, ten years later, no Citigroup executive has been indicted for these acts.[#] Bowen did not receive a whistleblower award because Citigroup wasn't fined based upon Bowen's testimony. (Citigroup was later fined.[3])

Robert Rubin wasn't going to stop Citigroup's plundering—as Treasury Secretary, he had been the driving force behind the two deregulatory bills that paved the way for the financial crisis. First came the 1999 repeal of the Glass-Steagall Act, the law that

Plunderer's Disguise: Wolves in Sheep's Clothing

separated savings banks from investment banks and insurance companies. Second came the Financial Services Modernization Act (FSMA), which made it illegal for states or the federal government to regulate derivatives. The repeal of the Glass-Steagall Act allowed Citibank to merge with Travelers Insurance. Rubin then joined the board of the merged company, renamed Citigroup, where he made $126 million. Then FSMA cleared the way for Citigroup and others to load up on derivatives that derived their value from high-risk mortgages. After the dust settled, Citigroup's recklessness required a $45 billion bailout and $306 billion in guarantees just to avoid bankruptcy.[3]

Rubin had created an image of being a "captain of industry" and man of integrity. He sprinted up the management ranks at Goldman Sachs to become co-CEO before being named U.S. Treasury Secretary by President Clinton. Rubin has received numerous honorary degrees from the most prestigious universities, including Harvard and Yale.

The only difference between Lay and Rubin was Rubin was too big to jail.

It's likely safe to say that Sharron Watkins and Richard Bowen are in the 25 percent of adults whose behavior is driven by internal morals. When faced with wrongdoing, they tried to stop it. But neither realized that they are in the minority of managers who will resist plundering. And the higher the level, the smaller the minority.[1] In contrast, plundering made Lay and

Rubin very rich. And the last thing they were going to do was kill the goose that laid the golden eggs.

Bottom Line: Beware the carefully manufactured images that allow plunderers to hide in plain sight.

Chapter 6

Plunderer's Revenge

"The last major accomplishment I want to mention is thanks to the efforts of the concurrent engineering team, led by Ed Minnock," announced Bruce, the company president, during a managers' meeting. "The new smaller tape drive is on track to ship on schedule and achieve all its goals."

Bruce added that past products had been late to market and riddled with quality problems. He emphasized how important it was to achieve the prescribed schedule and quality levels because commitments are made to customers months before the product begins shipping.

I was hired eleven months ago as the company's first concurrent engineering manager, and I led the group that designed supplier and production processes at the same time that product engineers designed the product. My goals were to reduce product development time and meet the manufacturing department's cost and quality goals. It seemed like they liked me here, and it was nice not to have to work every weekend.

The company used just-in-time production, which means that the company primarily relies upon local suppliers to deliver components to the production lines twice a day, minimizing the amount of inventory a company had to keep track of and store. Quality is the key to making just-in-time production work—if a suppliers' parts aren't free of defects, the production lines have to shut down. The company had achieved high enough quality from its local suppliers to hit its goal to produce at high volume.

When I returned to my office, there was an email from the engineering vice president. He had an opening for a project manager and encouraged me to apply for it. I thanked him but declined the offer. My boss, the second-level manufacturing engineering manager, had resigned recently and I had just applied for his job. I figured I had a good shot at the promotion because I had previously held the exact same position. Then the human resources department (HR) informed me that I couldn't interview for my former boss' job because I hadn't been with the company for a year. I asked if the one-year requirement could be waived since I was only one month short. HR told me that Clint, the manufacturing vice president and hiring manager for the position, could waive it.

I asked Clint to waive the requirement. He said no but invited me to be on the interview team. I reminded him that I held the exact same job at my previous company. Clint again invited me to be on the interview team. I agreed to be on the interview team.

There were three candidates, all outside hires. One was very good, one was acceptable, and the other was awful. The five members on the interview team recommended the very good candidate, but Clint wanted to hire the awful candidate because he would work for the lowest salary. I told Clint that his candidate had very little manufacturing experience and couldn't answer basic questions like, "How does manufacturing build quality into products?" The other members of the interview team provided similar input. Clint said he would take our input into consideration.

Clint hired the awful candidate, and I now had a new boss, Gomer.

The bad news kept piling up—the production prototypes of the new tape drive revealed a problem with a key supplier that made the component that allows the new tape drive to read tapes that were written on other tape drives. This was a critical component because our intended customers owned millions of tapes written on various other tape drives. And just like that, the new product was no longer on track to ship on schedule and achieve all its goals.

Because the company required high quality from its suppliers, we couldn't just ask the supplier to inspect 100 percent of its product and send us only parts that would work. Dave, the project manager in engineering, summoned me to his office to offer a potential solution, which was to switch to a contingency plan that would create an in-production process to fix the problem. If we did this, we would be able to ship on schedule and meet the quality goals, but we would miss the cost goal by a little.

I faced an ethical dilemma. Because of the commitments made to our customers, I had a responsibility to ship quality products on time. However, I also had a responsibility to make sure that my department, manufacturing, met its cost goals. And the manufacturing department paid the salary that fed my family. In this situation, the schedule, cost, and quality requirements were conflicting priorities, and I didn't know how to achieve all three. The below graphic outlines these competing goals.

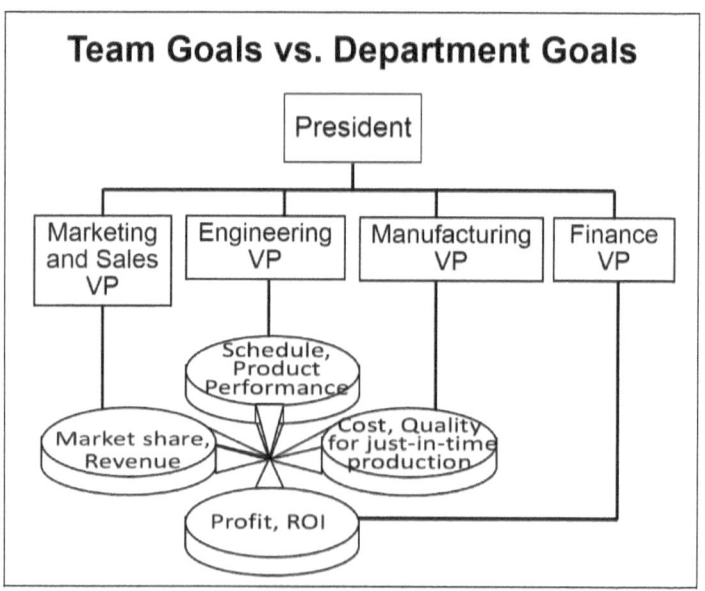

Plunderer's Revenge

I told Dave that I had to talk to my team before making a decision. To my surprise, my team was already working on Dave's contingency plan. I reminded them that we had to meet the department's cost goals. My team told me that Dave had already decided to switch to the contingency plan, and that they agreed with his decision. My dilemma intensified.

Next, I tried appealing to a higher authority—Gomer hadn't started yet, so I told Clint about the problem and the contingency plan. He literally said nothing. I took this lack of response to mean that he didn't consider this his problem. Since I was out of other options, I decided to go along with the contingency plan.

My team quickly developed an adjustment process that allowed the production line to achieve near perfect assemblies, but it also increased the cost of materials and labor, meaning that we would miss our cost goal. The product shipped on schedule, and Dave was congratulated for a job well done. The product was fairly successful: the revenue goal was nearly met, and customer satisfaction was the highest the company had seen. But the profit goal was missed because the cost goal was missed.

A few months later, I received my annual performance evaluation from Gomer. My ranking among managers dropped because I failed to achieve manufacturing's cost goal on the new product. I received zero credit for achieving the schedule and quality goals, and my annual raise was a paltry two percent. Gomer said that he and Clint decided that other managers, not me, would be the concurrent engineering managers on future product development projects. At the end of the meeting, Gomer asked how I thought he was doing in his new job. Rankled by my review, I told him the truth—that he wasn't qualified—which was not a smart move.

In the next staff meeting, Gomer announced that the manufacturing department was planning a layoff to reduce costs. He said that the layoff would be confined to manufacturing. He added that he had executed several layoffs at other companies and was very good at it. Great—a layoff right after the worst performance evaluation of my career, and right after I told my boss that he wasn't qualified for his job. I was not optimistic about my future at this company.

Bruce had spoken highly of the human resources vice president, Judy, so I sat down with her to discuss my problems. I told her about my performance review and that Gomer was unqualified. I asked if it would help my case to talk to Clint about Gomer.

Judy replied that top management was well aware of Gomer's incompetence and that she wasn't at all surprised by my performance review. She said that Clint valued loyalty above all else and spent most of his time covering his backside. She advised me against talking to Clint about Gomer. I then asked if it would help to talk to Bruce. Judy replied, "That would be career suicide. Bruce likes winners, not whiners." I thanked Judy for her honest advice. As I stood to leave,

Judy remarked that the last two people in my position were fired. From my meeting with Judy, I learned two things: Bruce was a wolf in sheep's clothing, and I needed to find a new job fast.

Desperate, I contacted Richard, the CEO at my previous company, to see if there were any openings available. Within days, the human resources department called and invited me to interview. When I arrived, the human resources manager told me that Hank had left, and that I was scheduled to interview with Hank's replacement. His replacement was a stark contrast to Hank—he was well dressed, polite, and professional. He told me that I could have my second-level manufacturing engineering manager job back. After the interview, I asked a few front-line people I used to work with how the atmosphere was now that Hank was gone. They all said it had gotten worse. I turned down the offer.

I contacted other people I had worked with at disk and tape drive companies. They were either working lots of overtime or looking for new jobs, but they were happy to hear from me—misery loves company. I had to find something new.

I saw an ad for a second-level manufacturing engineering manager. The contact person was a woman that had been a classmate of mine at Colorado State University's Master of Business Administration program. Although we hadn't talked since graduation, I called her about the position. She said that the second-level manufacturing engineering manager job was filled, but there was first-level manufacturing engineering manager job open. I paused to consider whether to apply for this lower-level position. As if sensing my uncertainty, she filled the silence by saying that the second-level manufacturing engineering manager was an excellent manager. That would be different. I decided to give it a try, and left the company just before the layoff began.

Chump

It never occurred to me that I would be punished for doing what was best for the company. I was wrong.

Although the company used cross-functional teams to develop new products, the team members were also responsible to their individual departments, and those departments' goals. When department goals competed, team members had to choose whether to work to meet the overarching team goals or the goals of the individual department. Not a fun choice to make.

On this project, the product development team considered two alternatives. The first achieved schedule and cost. The second achieved schedule and quality. Neither achieved all three. I supported the second alternative because those were the commitments that had already been made to customers. As a result, the engineering department achieved both of its goals: schedule and product performance. Manufacturing achieved one of its goals, quality to make just-in-time production work, but missed its cost goal.

Plunderer's Revenge

Clint gained his revenge by lowering my ranking and deciding that other managers, not me, would be would be the concurrent engineering managers on future product development projects. Like Rock in the previous chapter, I was punished for letting down my department. I was lucky to find a new job before being laid off.

Bottom line: Plunderers may harm you for doing what's best for the company, if it's not what's best for them.

Chapter 7

Playing the Game

"An important decision has been made for the new scanner you're responsible for," said Marilyn, my new boss as of three days ago. "It will be manufactured only in Singapore. Prototypes will still be built here, but all production will be built in Singapore."

The product was supposed to be the company's first high-volume scanner. The original plan was to build it in the Colorado design center, where engineers could quickly find and fix problems, and then transfer production to the Singapore facility once all the kinks had been ironed out.

This decision didn't make any sense—it was bad for everyone. Sure, labor was cheaper and the corporate tax rate was lower in Singapore, but ramping up production in Singapore would delay the product's introduction to market. This timing was critical because this new $399 scanner would replace the current, money-losing, $499 scanner. The current product was losing money because the original cost goal had been missed and the marketing department refused to raise the price since a higher price would reduce the company's market share for this product. This decision also meant the end of production in Colorado, which meant more of the company's local production team would be laid off.

In any event, the decision had been made, and I had to implement it. Because the product was a high-volume scanner and we'd experienced poor factory and field quality results in previous models, I had to make sure that both our component suppliers and the production processes we put in place were capable of building high quality parts. Marilyn allowed me to hire a few people to develop some testing and inspection protocols to ensure that we had better factor and field quality results this time around.

I soon learned that the most important decisions for the new scanner had already been made, and that these decisions added a lot of unnecessary costs. Fortunately, some of the product design engineers were open to lower-cost designs, and several high-cost metal parts could be redesigned into lower-cost plastic parts. But the worst decision made was to use a SCSI interface instead of a parallel interface. The SCSI interface cost $25 more and required customers to open their personal computers to install the SCSI printed circuit board. From my experience, only high-end users would install an interface board in their computers for slightly better performance; home and small business consumers wouldn't want to. This meant that this design decision would narrow the potential customer base interested in purchasing our new product, which is never a good idea.

I shared my concern with Marilyn and the rest of the project team. Although Marilyn agreed with me, no one on the project team did, so we went with the SCSI interface. My team scrambled to set up tools and processes to measure process capability just in time for the first prototype build. The results were not good: several processes were not capable of producing high quality products. And little improvement was made on the second, which was also the final, prototype build. Now the project was in trouble—we were nowhere near meeting the Six Sigma goals we had set for this product.

Gus, the project manager from the engineering department, told me that the Six Sigma goals must be sacrificed so the product could ship on schedule to replace the current, money-losing product. But sacrificing the Six Sigma goals would cause the product to miss its cost goal and increase the risk of defective units sneaking past our final tests and ultimately reaching customers. The benefit of achieving Six Sigma goals is that, because defective units aren't built, defective units aren't shipped. Ensuring that customers receive quality products boosts a company's reputation and customer satisfaction, which in turn leads to repeat customers and, through word of mouth or favorable reviews, new customers. New customers mean more revenue, and increased revenue leads to increased profits for the company as a whole.

It was two years later, but I found myself facing the exact same ethical dilemma with the same three competing goals: schedule, quality, and cost. I still didn't know how to achieve all three. But this time, I refused to compromise. I held firm to my position that we must meet the Six Sigma goals. I said as much to Marilyn, and then to her boss, the director of manufacturing. They were 100 percent supportive of my position. After a few relationship-damaging meetings between the engineering and manufacturing departments, Gus and his boss gave in.

The project was delayed so that we could make product and process design changes. To test the changes, the company built another production prototype in Colorado. This time there was good news: the Six Sigma goals were finally achieved.

My group and I traveled to Singapore to implement these processes and monitor their implementation by testing the resulting production prototypes. After two production prototype builds, the first-pass yield, or the number of units passing all tests and inspections on their first try divided by the total number of units going into the process, was over 90 percent, meaning that few units needed to be reworked, and the end-of-line quality audits yielded excellent results. Things were looking good.

The Singapore facility began production six weeks before the end of the fiscal year. But because of the delay to achieve the Six Sigma goals, and due the decision to only produce the product in Singapore, the product was scheduled for a February introduction and would miss the holidays, during which nearly half the year's entire volume was sold. This confirmed my belief that building only in Singapore was a big mistake.

But then the Singapore production line stepped on the gas. One hundred thousand units were built and shipped out of Singapore before the end of the fiscal year. Suddenly, $3 million in net profit from the new scanner was accrued in the fourth quarter, even though no units had been sold to customers. This had to be cooking the books. An accountant explained to me that Singapore tax law allowed the projected additional net profit from Singapore's lower corporate tax rate to be accrued as soon as the products left Singapore. Profit before sales—that's a nice accounting trick.

Thanks to the $3 million net profit accrual, the business achieved its net profit goal for the entire fiscal year. Management congratulated itself on its "brilliant" decision to manufacture only in Singapore. I suspect that top management made net profit the most important financial metric in order to expedite moving production to Singapore. But we didn't begin shipping the product to customers until February. And although the product exceeded all of its manufacturing goals, with first-pass yield rates and hardware quality at an all-time high, the product was a commercial failure. In addition to being late to market, a software installation glitch with the SCSI interface soon caused a flurry of calls from customers and returns. Soon retailers stopped promoting the product, and sales dropped.

Marilyn quickly assembled a team of software engineers from the engineering and manufacturing departments that solved the problem in a couple of weeks, saving the product from utter ruin. A reliability engineer had identified the cause of the software installation glitch months before the product shipped. During project meetings, the reliability engineer said it had the potential to be a big problem. But the engineering department refused to believe that it would be a problem, and their saying as much during these meetings frustrated the reliability engineer, who knew he wasn't being taken seriously.

I ignored the problem. Based on my previous experience, I knew that the engineering department would be blamed if it actually was a problem, so I didn't even mention it to Marilyn in our weekly update meetings. Instead, I focused on achieving the manufacturing's goals. By achieving manufacturing's goals, production cost was reduced by roughly $3 per unit. Yet the cost of the software glitch was ten times as much in lost sales alone. Sure enough, Gus was blamed for the software installation glitch. He would not lead another product development project at this company.

So how did it work out for me? I was promoted. Marilyn's boss left and Marilyn was promoted into his job. She then hired me into her old job. I was a second-level manufacturing engineering manager again.

Department Before Business?

With my experience from the last chapter fresh in mind, I made darn sure that my department's goals were achieved. I was fortunate to have a strong team that developed the supplier and production processes needed to produce excellent hardware quality. The Singapore production team did an excellent job of ramping up production with good quality. And, even though I ignored the software installation glitch that contributed to the product's failure, I was promoted. But this wasn't a very ethical choice—I knew the software glitch had the potential to harm customers and subsequently stockholders. And I had the power to do something about, yet I chose to do nothing. I violated the No Harm Principle.

I should have supported the reliability engineer and told Marilyn about the potential software installation glitch. Marilyn was the first boss I had who took responsibility for problems regardless of their origin or who would be blamed. She might have found a way to fix the software glitch before it harmed customers.

Bottom line: Taking care of only your department goals can help you individually even if your actions (or inactions) damage your company.

Chapter 8

Overconfidence Trap

The drinks were flowing, and the egos were growing. Thanks to my recent promotion, I received a last-minute invitation to an exclusive management retreat in Colorado's snow-covered mountains. During the cocktail hour preceding what would be an extravagant dinner, Brett, the general manager, welcomed us by announcing that this would be a great year. Brett became the general manager several months ago, while I was spending most of my time in Singapore, so this retreat was my first up close and personal encounter with him.

Brett radiated confidence. I had heard rumors that he was on the fast-track to top management in the company, perhaps even in line to become CEO. That evening, Brett was in a particularly good mood because he had just rolled out his new business strategy, which was, as he kept reiterating throughout the night, a great strategy.

After dinner, things took an odd turn. Several managers took turns heaping praise on Brett and his business strategy. But then some of the men started expressing how loyal they were to Brett. And a bizarre competition began among the managers—each man seemed intent on one-upping the previous man's claims of fealty. The winner was Roy, Brett's recent hire for the marketing director position. To prove his loyalty, Roy went outside in near-zero-degree weather to perform two dozen pushups in the snow. Upon his return, Brett rewarded Roy with a high five.

But there was a problem: Brett's business strategy was not great. In fact, I thought it was a disaster waiting to happen. There were two key elements to Brett's strategy: (1) regional manufacturing, that is, move half of the production operations from Singapore to Mexico, because Mexican labor was cheaper than Singaporean labor, and Mexico was closer to the American market; and (2) develop a $199 product that would match the competitors' current prices when it shipped in fifteen months. But the new $199 product would not be built in either Mexico or Singapore. Instead, it would be built by a Taiwanese company in Malaysia.

Brett's strategy was flawed for several reasons. First, our production volume was not high enough to cover the fixed cost of two factories now, and the production volume would decrease further when the new $199 product was built in Malaysia. Moreover, we didn't have extra people or money to bring a production facility in Mexico up to speed. Our business was under attack from government-funded, Taiwanese competition that had already driven the average price of scanners down 50 percent in the past year. Because of this competition, our company's market share had dropped from 45 percent to 28 percent. Revenue was flat, and profit had decreased. We needed every person and every dollar to go to the development of new products to profitably regain market share. Taiwan competitors weren't going to stand still for fifteen months so that we could catch up.

This was not a group lie. Brett believed he had developed a great strategy. Instead, this was **groupthink, a situation in which multiple people suspended their individual judgement in the face of incontrovertible evidence.** These managers were going along with Brett's claims that his strategy was great in order to stay in Brett's good graces.

Because I had ignored the customer dissatisfaction with the previous product to achieve my department's goals, I felt I had a responsibility to say something this time. I was facing another ethical dilemma: should I go along with the party line that Brett's strategy was great, or should I do something about it, even if doing so puts my career at risk? I decided that I had an obligation to tell Brett that competitors were going to clean our clock if we didn't develop competitive products at a low-end price points immediately. To mitigate some of the potential backlash, I planned to volunteer to lead a team to develop the low-end products.

I worked with our manufacturing people to prepare a competitive analysis that revealed that our production costs were 80 percent higher than multiple Taiwanese competitors' costs. I thought that would get Brett's attention. I bounced my plan off my boss Marilyn. Since falling backward out of my chair during the tape library fiasco, I learned to check with my boss before raising sensitive issues to higher ups. Marilyn thought Brett would listen to my concerns.

I outlined my key points and practiced my speech before meeting with Brett. My speech took all of two minutes. I had expected Brett to push back on my concerns, but he said nothing. Instead, he stood up from behind his desk, walked around to where I was sitting, and said, "Follow me." He led me down the hall and straight into the director of product design engineering's office. When the director looked up from his desk, Brett blankly stated, "Ed thinks our products aren't competitive," and walked away. I tried to retell my planned and practiced arguments. But unprepared for this turn of events, I stuttered and stammered my way through my previously polished assertions. When I finished, the director of product design engineering wordlessly turned back to his work. I slunk back to my desk. Needless to say, Brett had not taken me seriously. Neither had the director of product design engineering.

Afterwards, my attitude suffered. I vented my frustration with others. Before long, word got around to Marilyn. She called me into her office and told me that as a second-level manager, I needed to get on board with the company's strategy, especially with the decision to move manufacturing to Mexico. Marilyn had mentioned this before, but now she was serious. She said that Brett was tired of hearing about my criticism.

In response, I hotly retorted, "Are we [the manufacturing department] supposed to just blindly chase low-cost labor while engineering designs loser products that cause the business to fail and everyone to lose their jobs?" She shook her head. I continued to let loose, saying, "Why would engineering know how to develop low-cost products? They aren't familiar with the global supply base. We should be an equal partner in product development." Marilyn agreed, but then told me, again, that I needed to at least outwardly support the company's strategy.

The opportunity to vent made me feel better. I told Marilyn that several people in marketing also believed that Brett's strategy was a disaster waiting to happen. Then I asked if she knew who worked with Brett to develop his strategy. After a pause, she admitted that she was not involved. "Maybe engineering?" she said.

Because I appreciated Marilyn's efforts to keep me out of trouble, and because I wanted to keep my job, I stopped airing my grievances with Brett's strategy. Even so, after working for so many bad bosses, there were days when I came to work prepared to be fired.

Just a few days later, Jay, the marketing manager responsible for current products, invited me to a meeting. Once the meeting participants had assembled, Jay announced that he was going to propose lowering the price of our $399 product to $299 to stem the loss of market share. He explained that our market share was now under 25 percent and a Taiwanese company had replaced us as the market leader. He asked us to review his slide deck outlining his proposal and to join him in the meeting with the executives, because this was not going to be popular.

The meeting with the executives was tense. Initially, Brett was in denial—he wanted to know why the marketing department couldn't communicate the advantages of our $399 product over our competitors' products. Jay explained that our product's advantages were not worth an additional $200 to customers. During Jay's pitch to the executives, I couldn't help but notice that Jay's boss, Roy, was nodding at everything Brett said and grimacing at anything Jay said. I involuntarily replayed the image of Roy doing pushups in the snow during the manager retreat—his reaction was not surprising.

After Jay finished his presentation, Brett proposed dropping the price to $349. Jay calmly and professionally maintained that we have to lower the price to $299 because $299 is the highest price that retailers will carry. After a protracted and painful discussion, Brett reluctantly approved the price drop.

I understood why Brett was reticent to approve the price drop, as it meant that the company would miss its profit goal for the second half of the fiscal year. This product was simply not profitable when sold at $299. Fortunately, the business had another product that was profitable, an $800 bursting-with-technology scanner.

Overconfidence Trap

Jay's plan backfired: within days of our dropping the price to $299, several Taiwanese competitors dropped their prices to $99. The difference was $200 again. Worse, $99 was an impulse-buy price point, meaning that customers would be even more likely to purchase our competitor's product over ours. Sure enough, our market share was soon down to 20 percent. I was tempted to tell Brett that this was what "cleaning our clock" looked like. I refrained.

Things got worse: the Singapore group notified us that all the net profit booked on hundreds of thousands of unsold units assuming the price would be $399 had to be written down because there was no profit at $299. Now the scanner business will suffer a net profit loss for the second half of the year.

And the hits just kept on coming: the project team working on the new $199 product announced that it would miss its scheduled release date. Although the team in Mexico had gotten that facility's production up and running, the production schedules for both the Mexico and Singapore production facilities were reduced.

I was living in the Twilight Zone, and kept my resume updated.

I ran into a very happy Brett in the hallway. He asked me how things were going. I requested that we talk in private. After he agreed, I told him: "We just spent a lot of time and money bringing up a production facility that we don't need while our market share fell to 20 percent and now we're losing money. Wouldn't it have been smarter to use those people and that money to develop competitive new products?"

"I see your point," Brett replied, seemingly unfazed by my criticism. I soon found out why Brett was so happy—he had just received a big promotion and was one step closer to the coveted corner office.

A few days later, Jay announced that he had accepted a similar position at another company. I asked him to stay, reminding him that Brett was leaving, but Jay said he was tired of working for a man whose most memorable contribution was doing pushups in the snow.

Overconfidence Trap

The overconfidence trap occurs when unwarranted confidence produces preventable mistakes. The greater the unwarranted confidence, the bigger the mistakes. Leaders fall into the overconfidence trap when unwarranted confidence prevents them from considering multiple alternatives and listening to feedback, particularly critical feedback.

Brett can't be blamed for accepting promotions. But he can be blamed for disregarding evidence that his business strategy was deeply flawed and for using his position of authority to pressure people to agree with him. The business became unprofitable as a result.

Brett either didn't want to consider the possibility that he was wrong or didn't want to admit that he made a big mistake. Admitting errors and mistakes can result in lost credibility and career cost. And the higher

Overconfidence Trap

up a person is in an organization, the higher the cost.[1] Unwarranted confidence is particularly common among executives in the tech industry. In one experiment, tech executives were given a quiz about the tech industry. The executives predicted that 95 percent of their answers were correct, when actually just 20 percent of their answers were correct.[2]

Bottom Line: Unwarranted confidence may be an advantage when seeking a job, but is more often than not a disadvantage when doing a job.

Chapter 9

An Ethical Team Saves the Day

"Market share is down to 18 percent. Revenue is declining and you're all hemorrhaging money." The Senior Vice President glared at me and the other managers in the room. "Next year, you will be shutting down this business." Those were the final words of a depressing quarterly business review. Three hundred jobs hung in the balance.

After the meeting, finger pointing was rampant. The engineering department was blamed for designing uncompetitive products. The marketing team was blamed for failing to effectively communicate the advantages of our products. And the manufacturing folks were blamed for failing to reduce cost enough to turn a profit. We desperately needed profitable products priced at the low-end of the market.

With Brett gone, Marilyn was designated the acting general manager—a classic example of the glass cliff. The term "glass cliff" refers to the practice of giving women leadership roles when businesses are failing. If

An Ethical Team Saves the Day

Marilyn failed, she wouldn't get another chance at such a senior role.

With the business facing near-certain failure, Marilyn was ready to try something different. She posted, and I applied for a business team manager position, which involved building a profitable business at the low end of the market. It had an exhaustive interview process.

Vern, the director of product design engineering, opened the first-round interview with a brain-teaser: I'm in a canoe on a lake. There's a rock in the canoe. If I throw the rock overboard and it sinks to the bottom of the lake, what happens to the water level in the lake? I asked why there was a rock in a canoe. He told me to answer the question. I got it wrong. Vern explained that the lake level falls because the density (mass / volume) of the rock alone is greater than the density of the water. Next Vern asked me a few technical questions that I didn't know the answers to. Finally, he asked what I thought of "followership." For months, Vern had been complaining about employees that question the business plan rather than applying all their energy into blindly implementing it. Vern probably thought I didn't put much stock in followership. I may have proved him right, because I replied that the key to getting people to follow you is having a plan that's worth following.

Next up in the interview process was a meeting with Roy, the marketing director. He told me Marilyn asked him for input for my annual performance evaluation and he wanted me to hear it straight from him. Gleefully, he said that I remind him of breaking glass. When I asked what that meant, he said that it means I'm overly critical and disruptive. I got the sense that this interview was not going very well. Roy then asked me a few questions about how our products were marketed and sold. I told him what I knew, which was that a lot of our sales were in retail big-box stores.

It was clear that neither Roy nor Vern thought I was qualified for the job. I didn't know much about the technology used in scanners. I didn't know much about how scanners were marketed and sold. And I was a troublemaker. Despite these flaws, Marilyn hired me. It helped to be the only one that applied for a position.

When teams try to do something that has never been done before, there are two factors critical for success: building an ethical team and eliminating external threats. Eliminating external threats is necessary to create a supportive environment for that team to operate in.

The key to building an ethical team is ensuring that team members commit to each other's success as well as their own success. Trust built from that commitment produces the confidence required to take on hard problems and collaborate until solutions are found that achieve everyone's goals. It's the only way to avoid the ethical dilemma of having to choose between valid, yet competing, goals of supporting their individual department or the company as a whole. Without the

An Ethical Team Saves the Day

confidence that commitments are shared, team members tend to retreat back to the safety of promoting only their department's goals, where they will be welcomed with open arms until the business fails and everyone is laid off.

The principal external threat, in this instance, was resistance to change. A few key managers, including Vern, were so proud of the bursting-with-technology products designed for high-tech users that they saw no reason to make products for non-technical, cost-conscious customers. They couldn't be allowed to obstruct the team's low-end efforts.

Realizing that this team faced a difficult task, I asked Marilyn for advice. Marilyn had a knack for building effective teams. She knew that the right combination of individuals can accomplish miracles, and that one out-of-sync team member can cause the group dynamic to break down into defensive, unproductive behavior, which almost always results in an accomplish of zilch.

Heeding Marilyn's advice, I met with each department director and requested a specific person for my team. Roy, the marketing director, and the directors of manufacturing and finance assigned me the first-level managers I had cherry-picked for my cause. Vern did not. Instead he assigned a manager that had just resigned and would be leaving the company in three weeks.

Top management handed down the goals for my low-end business for the following year: $200 million in revenue at 5 percent profit. Although we were entering an ultra-competitive low-end market, I was told it was imperative that we meet the profit goal.

In our first meeting, I asked the team members to share their vision of the end product, the goals they were tasked with meeting, and why they wanted to be on the team. I've found that giving people a chance to be heard prepares them to listen.

Cheryl, the marketing team member, said it was frustrating to watch our market share fall from 45 percent to 18 percent. She added that half of the revenue worldwide is from products priced under $200, and we don't have any products priced under $200. She wanted three products priced at $199, $149, and $99 to regain market leadership, and set a goal to get our market share back in the 30+ percent range.

Rob from the finance department said he wanted to achieve at least 7 percent profit because that was the average for the company. Mick from engineering said that his number one goal was to release the product on schedule. On previous new products, the engineering department had been thrown curve balls, like the addition of complicated last-minute features, which threw them off the prescribed timeline.

Cheryl shared that her top priority was to produce a $99 product because our competitors had been selling products at that price point for nearly a year. Our lowest-priced product was still $299. Bill, the manufacturing guy, helpfully presented an analysis demonstrating that the company couldn't profitably

An Ethical Team Saves the Day

ship an empty box for $99. We were all embarrassed by past quality problems, so we immediately set a goal of garnering industry-leading customer satisfaction.

We began brainstorming for solutions, but the ramifications of the financial situation sunk in. For years I'd been itching to design a complete new low-cost product: hardware and software. But we didn't have the people or the money we needed to do it.

From my interviews, I knew that top management expected us to purchase entire products, add third-party software, and then slap our company's logo on them. This approach required the fewest people and least money. But Cheryl was 100 percent opposed to this idea—she said customers would not be fooled, and we would not meet our handed-down goals, much less the goal of 30+ percent market share.

We needed to try something new. Months ago, a software engineer had suggested that we purchase hardware and integrate it with our software. I bounced this idea off the team members. The more this option was discussed, the more potential it seemed to have. It was certainly better than the alternative pushed by top management. But we had concerns—we had never tried this approach. No one in the industry had.

There was some serious risk involved. This approach required the engineering department to figure out how to achieve good performance and image quality with purchased hardware. Some engineers thought that was impossible. And this approach required the manufacturing department to significantly reduce cost across the entire supply chain. It also required me talking the top brass into giving us a small software development team to develop a user experience so superior that customers would pay a premium for our products. Despite the risks, we all agreed to explore this option.

We found common ground and agreed on team goals: 30+ percent market share, 7+ percent profit, and industry-leading customer satisfaction. We were able to reach consensus on these goals because no one person's goals were traded off. No one said, "Get real. We can't achieve 30 percent market share at 7 percent profit. Stop talking about it." Team chemistry was good.

I met with Marilyn, explained our plan, and asked for the required staff and funding. She told me to come back with a complete proposal—one that included proof that our approach would succeed.

Hand-picking my team now paid off—Cheryl, an expert in consumer-centric design, was our secret weapon. She had already figured out exactly what the target customers wanted to do with this product, and she had tested it with customers. Using Cheryl's knowledge about what the customer wanted, we worked backwards to define the product, its features, and the technology needed to implement it. Right off the bat, we knew that we had a product that was easier to use than our current $299 product.

Six of us traveled to Taiwan to seek out companies that could sell us hardware at a price low enough to beat our competitors in the marketplace. The manufacturing department had received quotes from these same companies before on similar hardware—none were at the price point we needed. Moreover, we had to convince these companies that we were not trying to spy on their operations but were serious about buying hardware from them.

Before the trip, we sent requests for quotes and prototypes to nine prospective suppliers. Mick found an intern to test whether the prototypes worked with our software. That's when we received a first bout of good news: some combinations of competitor hardware and our software worked fairly well together—now we knew our idea stood a chance.

When we landed in Taipei, we were greeted by the Sunday newspaper headlines, which announced the death of our business due to a sound trouncing from Taiwanese scanner companies. Not deterred by this news, we spent the next seven consecutive days negotiating with and evaluating suppliers. That's when we got our second bout of good news: all nine suppliers used clean rooms to build scanners, and three quoted us prices low enough to profitably price our lowest priced product at $129. We paid special attention to how workers were treated as we evaluated each supplier—we couldn't afford to be associated with any sweatshops.

The night before we left, we met in a conference room at the hotel to come to a decision regarding the supplier. Mick said that, given the lack of staff and funding, the engineering department could produce, at maximum, two new products. And the only way engineering could develop two products was to use the market leader and our toughest competitor for both, because only the market leader had the technical skills required to build the hardware we needed. Bill opposed using any competitor for more than one product because of the risk involved—the competitor could cause our products to fail, by withholding supply or shipping us hardware with quality problems. Yet not using a competitor for both products would mean that we could only develop one product—one product would not meet our handed-down goals, much less our team goals.

I was facing another ethical dilemma, but this time around I made the right decision. Although it was late, we'd been putting in long hours, and everyone was tired, I urged the team to keep searching for a solution. I did not want to leave Taiwan without a plan.

Four hours later, we had a breakthrough: use the market leader for the $129 product, and a small non-competitor with good technical capability for a product priced at $199. The small company had been eliminated earlier due to its lack of production capacity, but it had just enough capacity for a $199 product. We had again found common ground.

Now the team had a plan: produce two products, not three; use two suppliers, not one; and hit a price point of $129, not $99. None of these options were any one department's first choice, but all team members supported it. We remained committed to a 30+ percent

An Ethical Team Saves the Day

market share and a 7+ percent profit.

The week following the Taiwan trip was a whirlwind. I blocked off two hours during the following Monday's executive staff meeting, but needed an iron-clad proposal so we could get top management's approval and start development. The clock was ticking.

Cheryl worked with the marketing team to prepare a sales forecast. Great news: it showed the two products, as defined, would easily beat our handed-down goals of $200 million in revenue at 5 percent profit. With Mick gone, I met with Vern and asked for the same first-level engineering manager I asked for before. He offered someone else. I refused. Without an engineering team member, I asked a second-level software engineering manager if he could organize a working-prototype demonstration. Thankfully, he agreed and scheduled it for Thursday.

In our weekly team meeting, we had a serious discussion about what could go wrong. Bill, from Manufacturing said he was very worried that the market leader would not perform. He proposed that we have a well-developed contingency plan to switch to another competitor for the $129 product if needed. Fortunately, the cost would be minimal and Bill's team would do most of the work. We agreed to move forward with the contingency plan. We also agreed that the biggest risk was Vern and Roy. They could easily obstruct our efforts by either withholding the people we needed or reassigning people from our project to other projects. They could also veto funding or delay important decisions.

That Thursday, there was a demonstration of the working prototypes. The demo, which was conducted by the same intern who had tested the prototypes for us, was well attended, particularly by the engineering department, and everyone agreed that technical feasibility had been proven.

With the meeting with executives just days away, I agonized over how to overcome the demonstrated resistance to change. Vern had refused, without explanation to give me the first-level manager that I asked for twice already. Clearly, he was not going to do me any favors.

Vern, Roy, and others refused to accept the fact that the business would be shut down unless revenue and profit increased. They were living somewhere between anger and denial, but they certainly weren't taking responsibility for the success of the business or the livelihoods of its 300 employees.

I came up with a plan: set up a temporary organization with my own budget and small marketing and engineering teams reporting to me. Because this would be controversial, I met with Marilyn before presenting it in Monday's executive meeting. After a lengthy discussion, she agreed to support my plan, but told me that I would have to post the marketing and engineering management jobs business-wide and conduct a thorough interview process. We were cutting it close.

An Ethical Team Saves the Day

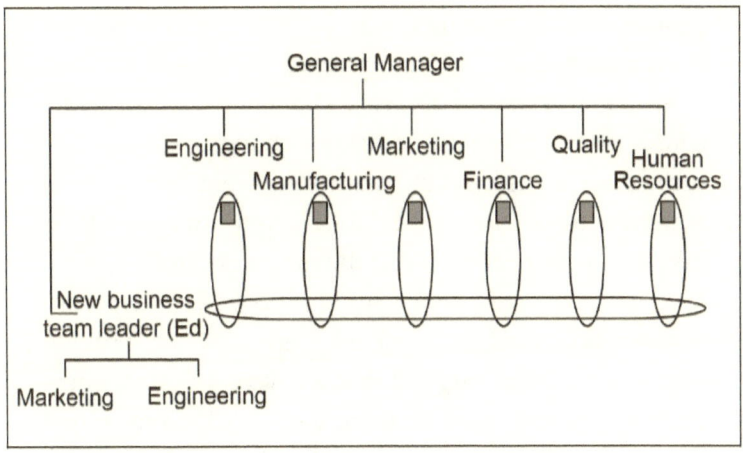

Monday's two-hour meeting with the top executives turned into an all-day affair. I began the meeting by announcing that we had achieved technical, market, and financial feasibility, and if given approval today, we could ship two products in seven months. I explained that we couldn't meet our goals by purchasing products and putting our company logo on them, and that the only way to meet our goals was to purchase hardware and combine it with our software. I presented the test results showing the products' good performance and image quality as well as the marketing forecast showing $250 million in revenue at 7 percent profit. The room was all smiles. Then I presented the procurement details.

The smiles quickly faded—none of the executives wanted to use the market leader as a supplier. I explained that I didn't want to rely on the market leader for the hardware either, but the only path to a profitable $129 product was by using the hardware from a competitor and the market leader had the best quality and technical ability. I explained that we had a contingency plan to quickly change to another competitor if the market leader didn't perform. After a lengthy discussion, the executives offered their lukewarm support for using the market leader.

Then I presented my proposed temporary organization. And, as expected, Vern and Roy strongly opposed the idea. I argued that we were building a new business model, one that served a different target customer, the cost-conscious customer, and that a small temporary organization would enable the new business to succeed without disrupting the current business that catered to high-tech customers.

Vern and Roy argued that they were better situated to support all of the new products, including the low-end product, because they could bring the depth and breadth of their organizations' skills to bear. The debate dragged on for hours. I kept coming back to the argument that a small temporary organization would enable the new business to succeed without disrupting the current business. Marilyn and the four other executives nodded in agreement since the last thing they wanted was for both the current and the new businesses to fail. Vern and Roy weren't buying it.

Marilyn wanted consensus. I knew that wasn't likely. Finally, Marilyn announced that we would move forward with the temporary organization, and asked the executives if they would support my proposal.

An Ethical Team Saves the Day

They all said they would.

She requested that my team and I provide weekly updates to the executives in her staff meeting. She further stipulated that any major changes to our plan, such as changes to prices or product definitions, would have to be approved by the executives. I was relieved—given Roy and Vern's attitudes, I wasn't sure whether we'd get the approval we needed. In just four weeks, my team had developed a proposal, achieved project feasibility, and gained the executives' approval to proceed with development.

I wrote job descriptions for the two managers I was now empowered to hire; the requirements emphasized teamwork experience and other soft skills such as active listening. Teamwork was more critical than ever now, given that the relationship between the engineering and marketing departments had become quite adversarial.

I hired Paul Beiser (real name), the first-level engineering manager I had requested twice from Vern. Paul was the last piece of the ethical team puzzle. I also hired Cheryl, whose successful consensus building and expertise in customer needs had been instrumental in getting the project approved by the executives. Bill and Rob also remained on the team, but they continued to report to their departments.

Developing two new products, with two new suppliers, at the same time resulted in a truckload of problems. As I had hoped, Paul worked effectively with the marketing and manufacturing departments; he also used expertise from the engineering department to quickly solve problems. Despite the challenges we were facing, the team remained committed to achieving all the project goals: market share, revenue, customer satisfaction, profit, cost, on-time delivery, etc. We stuck to our commitment to not trade off one goal to achieve another. With this commitment, and this consensus, every team member remained resolute—no one retreated to her or his department for support in trading off another department's goals.

As Marilyn had predicted, the team was able to perform miracles. Cheryl's marketing people worked with Paul's software engineers to develop user-friendly, one-button, one-click tasks. The software engineers also improved product performance and image quality.

The manufacturing department supply chain staff set a goal to reduce the total supply chain cost in half: distribution, localization, returns, customer support, and repair. Ruth, the manager, and her team used a just-in-time approach to accomplish this goal. For current products, finished goods were shipped from Asian factories to regional distribution centers around the world in bulk packs that were inventoried, repackaged into finished goods packaging with localized software, re-inventoried, and finally shipped to retailers. This was costly and wasteful. Ruth's team designed multi-language finished goods packaging and set up the hardware suppliers to package our product

An Ethical Team Saves the Day

in finished goods packaging in Asia, cutting out the cost, waste, and extra handling associated with the bulk pack.

Similar breakthroughs were made in returns, customer support, and repair. With these efficiencies in place, our lowest priced product could be profitably priced at $99.

We met with the executives to propose the price drop. They were initially skeptical, which was understandable considering the business hadn't met a quarterly profit goal in over two years. They conservatively proposed that we introduce the product to market at $129 and drop the price later, if profit was high enough. After a protracted debate, Rob, our finance team member, successfully persuaded the executives to approve the price change. Considering that we couldn't ship an empty box profitably at $99 four months earlier, this was quite the accomplishment.

With the price drop approval in hand, Cheryl promoted the heck out of the $99 product. The two products were shipped to customers on schedule. Together they earned $320 million in revenue at 15 percent profit, with industry-leading customer satisfaction. Competitors dropped their lowest priced products to $79 and $89. However, because customers loved our one-button, one-click tasks, they were happy to pay a little more for our products. We regained market leadership and touted a 35 percent share. The market leader became a reliable supplier. Employees were proud of their accomplishments.

The temporary organization allowed our team to successfully build a new business while minimizing disruption to the existing business. Given the minimal disruption, the existing business developed three packed-with-technology products on schedule.

The scanner business was no longer in danger of closing; in fact, it went on to win that year's President's Quality Award, an award given to the business within the company with the most outstanding performance. When the President's Quality Award committee met with my team and asked us to identify factors that caused the project to far exceed its goals, Cheryl immediately handed all the credit to the other team members and their departments. Other team members followed suit. At first, the committee members didn't know how to react. Then the committee leader announced that this is how teams are supposed to work together.

Because the team members worked together to ensure each other succeeded, my job was actually fairly easy—and it was the most fun I've had at work. This ethical team enabled me to succeed, even though I didn't know much about technology or marketing. I was promoted to director. Cheryl was promoted. Paul took on a new role focusing on researching new products. The word "acting" was dropped from Marilyn's title.

Ethical Teams

Five elements are needed to build an ethical team:[1]

An Ethical Team Saves the Day

1. A noble mission or purpose;
2. Interdependent team members;
3. Needed skills;
4. Commitment to everyone's success, rather than individual success; and
5. A supportive environment.

The scanner team had a noble purpose—build a large profitable business at the ultra-competitive, low end of the scanner market fast. If we didn't accomplish this mission, the scanner business would have been shut down, and 300 people would have lost their jobs.

Developing new products is an interdependent process. The Marketing team can't specify a better product than the engineering team can design. And the engineers can't design a better product than the manufacturing folks can build. Product specification, product design, and manufacturing decisions need to be made at the same time because they effect each department.

The key to building an ethical team is hiring people with needed skills, who are willing to commit to everyone's success, and a supportive environment. This team took on audacious goals (30+ percent market share, 7+ percent profit, etc.) and searched outside of the traditional methods of operation until solutions were found that met or exceeded everyone's needs.

This team also identified what could go wrong and took actions to reduce the risks, including a contingency plan in the event the market leader didn't perform and a temporary organization.

Marilyn created the supportive environment we needed to succeed. If I hadn't been allowed to set up a temporary organization, staffed with people with the needed technical and teamwork skills, we wouldn't have obtained such successful results. Marilyn also encouraged me to collaborate with the executives, rather than try to keep our activities secret. By providing weekly updates to the executives, they felt like they had control over the project, and responded by helping us rather than stymieing our efforts. Had I fallen into the trap of battling with the executives for control over the project, the team wouldn't have succeeded.

Bottom line: Teams made up of the right combination of individuals, operating in a supportive environment, can accomplish miracles

Ethical Team Power

The table summarizes the results of the four product development projects described in chapters 5, 6, 7, and this chapter, as well as my and other team members' behaviors.

In chapter 5, Rock and I both pursued our department goals, at the expense of the each other's department goals, a lose-lose arrangement. Rock was fired because he reversed his position and decided the tape libraries were not ship-worthy, after maintaining for months that they were, even though his reversed

An Ethical Team Saves the Day

decision was the right choice to make. I kept my job because I had maintained all along that the libraries were not ship-worthy and did a better job of defending my department's goals, although I did get into trouble with Hank and Richard.

Department vs. Business

Other guy's priority

		Department Goals	All Project Goals
My priority	All Project Goals	Chapter 6: Tape drive 1. Product is fairly successful 2. Other guy's department goals met, mine missed. 3. I'm punished. 4. Dave is congratulated. 5. Lose - win	Chapter 9: Ethical team 1. All goals exceeded. 2. Everyone is rewarded. 3. Win - win
	Department Goals	Chapter 5: Tape libraries 1. Tape libraries are recalled 2. Schedule goal met, all other goals missed. 3. I'm in trouble. 4. Rock is fired. 5. Lose – lose	Chapter 7: Scanner 1. Revenue, profit, customer satisfaction goals missed 2. My department goals met, other guy's missed. 3. I'm rewarded. 4. Gus is punished. 5. Win - lose

In chapter 6, I did what I thought was right for the company: achieve schedule with good quality because commitments had already been made to customers. By doing what I thought was right, I helped the engineering department achieve its schedule and product performance goals, but caused Manufacturing to miss its cost goal. Dave, the engineering manager's career advanced. I was punished because the manufacturing vice president cared more about cost

Teams vs. Plunderers

than satisfying customers.

In chapter 7 (lower right box), I did not do what was right for the company. I did what I thought was right for my department and was promoted after achieving my department's goals, while ignoring a product design defect that caused the product to miss its revenue, profit, and customer satisfaction goals. This time my career advanced. Gus, the engineering manager, was punished because the engineering department missed its schedule and product performance goals.

At these three companies, my individual success was at odds with the company's success. The problem with reward systems like these is that they can cause the company as a whole to suffer. In fast-moving industries, like technology, a few failed new products can ruin a company.

In this chapter (upper right box), I was able to build an ethical team, with Marilyn's help. Ethical team members worked considerably harder to find solutions that met everyone's goals than the teams did in chapters 5, 6, and 7. This diligence paid off as the project exceeded all its goals, stressful ethical dilemmas were avoided, and everyone was rewarded.

Bottom line: When a part of a highly interdependent team, in which team members' goals compete, all team members must be committed to each other's goals along with their own goals. If they aren't, it's in each individual's best interest to focus

An Ethical Team Saves the Day

on his department goals, even if doing so hurts the company as a whole. Therefore, companies should review their department versus business reward structures and align rewards with business success.

Chapter 10

Building Consensus

"$30 million write off," announced Lisa, the finance manager. "That's on top of the $70 million the digital camera business was expected to lose this year." After these announcements, the room was looking pretty grim.

"Are you confident that this write down will cover all the price drops the sales force needs to sell all the finished goods inventory left over from the holiday selling season?" Marilyn asked Lisa.

"Yes, assuming the price drops happen right away. Cameras lose value very quickly. I have a timeline."

"So now we're looking at $200 million in revenue and a $100 million loss for this year?" I asked.

"Yes."

The three of us stared silently at the numbers, thinking the same thing, "This looks really bad."

"What's the next step?" Lisa asked.

"Next week I meet with the CEO and the senior executives to try to talk them into letting the digital camera business continue," Marilyn said.

Building Consensus

Now that the scanner business had been successfully turned around, top management decided to give the failing digital camera business to Marilyn—another glass cliff challenge for her. She asked me to lead the camera business just before the holidays.

Marilyn made three trips to the West Coast over the next two months to plead our case. Somehow, she persuaded senior management and the CEO to let the camera business continue. She also talked them out of conducting a layoff, which was the customary punishment when profit goals are missed. A layoff would have been a death blow, as we recently went through a company-wide layoff and our competitors were outspending us by 10 to one. But when it came to building consensus, Marilyn was the master. Top management had a message for Marilyn and me: last chance. If the camera business doesn't turn a profit next year, it will be shut down.

The first thing I did was hire Paul Beiser. Some people perform under pressure; others don't. Paul performs. The pressure was on. Our current business plan had to work, or we were done.

Bad news: our business plan didn't last three months. Our sales team reported that retailers told them that Sony and Canon were planning to introduce five megapixel cameras just before the holiday season next year, which ran from Thanksgiving to New Years. This was the time of year when half of the entire year's volume of digital cameras were sold. As a result, the price of our flagship new product, a four-megapixel, 3X optical zoom camera, which was scheduled to ship in nine months, would have to be lowered from $499 to $399 before the holidays.

This caused a big problem: at $499, the four-megapixel camera was very profitable. At $399, it covered the variable costs but not the fixed cost. It still made sense to sell it at $399, but it was not profitable, and we were counting on this camera to deliver much of the revenue needed to turn a profit next year.

This was a big surprise: We bought nearly all of our sensors from Sony, yet Sony had told us that its five megapixel sensors would be available after the holidays, not before. I sent Bill, the same excellent procurement manager from last chapter, to Japan to meet with Sony. Sony confirmed that it planned to introduce five megapixel cameras before the holidays next year, but five megapixel sensors would not be supplied to us until after the holidays. Adding insult to injury, Sony also informed Bill that our supply of four mega-pixel sensors would be cut in half, until Sony began building five megapixel sensors. This meant that sales of our four-megapixel, 3X optical zoom camera would be severely constrained, and that we would miss our new revenue and profit goals for this year. It was too late to change to another sensor supplier. Now we had a disaster on our hands.

After several unproductive phone calls with Sony's U.S. management, I invited executives from Sony Japan

Building Consensus

to San Diego so Marilyn and her boss, the executive vice president, could plead our case. It didn't help. Sony's newly appointed executive responsible for sensor allocation explained that demand for its best-in-industry sensors was higher than planned. Then he matter-of-factly and without a hint of remorse told us that Sony's first priority was equipping its own cameras with sensors, followed closely by a second priority commitment to provide sensors to companies that sold Sony other key components. Sony's second priority was Canon because Canon sold lenses to Sony. Third priority was reserved for any Japanese company that wanted sensors. As we were a distant fourth priority, we were effectively locked us out of the five-megapixel sensor market for the holidays.

Now we were in trouble. As word spread that this-year's and next-year's business plans had already crumbled, rumors that the camera business would be shut down began to circulate once more. A senior finance executive informed me that the camera business was not in the following year's budget. A marketing executive told the North American sales force not to waste their time selling cameras because the business won't be around for long.

I was stressed. I did not want to be responsible for the camera business closing and everybody losing their jobs. I held an all-hands meeting to explain that we desperately needed a very profitable camera. I asked for ideas—they poured in. They would all help but not enough.

Teams vs. Plunderers

A couple of weeks later, Dave, an engineer and photographer, proposed a consumer big-zoom camera: four megapixels, 8X optical zoom, priced at $499, which would use the same four-megapixel sensor used in our 3X optical zoom camera. Dave had approached Fujinon, an optics company, and Fujinon agreed to build a custom lens. Fujinon was a subsidiary of Fujifilm, a competitor. At the time, most big-zoom cameras contained large sensors, large lenses, and price tags around $1,000.

The next hurdle was sensors. To have any chance of developing the big-zoom camera in time for a fall introduction, we had to leverage the firmware from the four megapixel, 3X optical zoom camera, which meant that we had to use four mega-pixel sensors from Sony. Bill, our procurement manager, again traveled to Japan. We received our first break—Sony was willing to provide additional four megapixel sensors beginning in September, after Sony began production of five megapixel sensors for itself and other Japanese camera companies. Bill was careful not to let Sony know that we were developing a big-zoom camera.

The two key questions were: (1) would customers buy our four megapixel, big-zoom camera instead of five megapixel, 3X optical zoom camera from established industry heavyweights, and (2) could we develop a high quality, profitable big-zoom camera in time for the holiday season next year.

A small team was quickly put together to find answers to these questions. The team found a supplier

Building Consensus

for an electronic view finder and a contract manufacturer that would build it. We prepared a product development plan—the technical risk was high, and the schedule was tight.

The marketing team prepared a forecast. Bad news: it only predicted $40 million in revenue. At $40 million in revenue, there was no profit. The big-zoom camera needed at least $60 million in revenue to make its profit goal of 7 percent. The big-zoom camera did not appear to be feasible from a technical, market, or financial standpoint. A few managers told me that moving forward would be irresponsible. Some even called our idea "a product without a market".

This decision was my responsibility. Marilyn was recently promoted to senior vice president and had taken on additional responsibilities. She was traveling a lot, and we didn't talk much anymore. The bottom line was that if we didn't develop the big-zoom camera, the camera business would miss next year's profit goals and be shut down, resulting in everyone losing their jobs. If we did develop the big-zoom camera, the business might live to see another day.

The x-factors: Dave and other engineers wanted to make this camera. More importantly, Paul, their boss, wanted to make this camera. I knew that team would do whatever it took to succeed. I decided to go for it. Paul was given the green light to proceed.

Given the risk and controversy surrounding this decision, I spent a lot of time explaining the rationale behind my decision. Many people thought I was nuts.

Teams vs. Plunderers

I assembled a development team. Our marketing manager contacted the marketing and sales people around the world and informed them of our new plan. Asia and North America said, "Okay." Europe responded, "No thanks." I was stunned. We sold over half our cameras in the European market. Without Europe on board, the big-zoom camera would be a product without a market. I asked our marketing manager why Europe declined our new product. He replied, "Europe didn't say no. Europe just hasn't said yes yet." I asked him what the plan was to convince them to take the camera. He said I'd be going to Europe to talk them into it.

It was my turn to build consensus.

When I arrived at the marketing center in Germany, I met three young guys who were responsible for European region's digital camera sales. Before we finished introducing ourselves, they informed me that our cameras were awful. I spent a week in Germany and Switzerland and met many of the European sales staff. They all told me our cameras were awful. This was at odds with what we were telling ourselves back at headquarters. I asked for more information—what makes our cameras so awful? The three young guys were happy to inform me that the main complaint was the camera's design. I was confused, so they showed me cameras known for their design; they compared these cameras' features to our cameras' features, in detail. These guys had done their homework.

I asked why they said no to a consumer big-zoom

Building Consensus

camera. They said they were afraid that we would design another awful-looking camera, and they didn't want to sell any more awful-looking cameras. Since these guys obviously knew what they were talking about, I asked if they would help us design it. This camera was not in the original business plan. My plan was to have engineers wing it—not a great plan. The three young guys liked the idea. They introduced me to their boss and just before I left, their boss assigned a designer to our team. Our biggest critics were now the newest members of our team.

The chemistry between the European designer, the European marketing team, and Paul's team was phenomenal. The camera design was breathtaking.

But the schedule was still a problem. I turned to our supply chain team for a solution. Previously, our finished goods were packaged in Asian factories and shipped by water to distribution centers, where it was inventoried and then trucked to stores, which meant that it took six weeks for the product to travel from the factories in Asia to the stores in North America and Europe. A supply chain staff analysis revealed that 80 percent of North America sales were concentrated in just five big-box retail stores. Europe was similarly situated. The supply chain team proposed that we ship by air directly to these big-box retail store warehouses, which would both cut out the distribution centers and six weeks off the schedule. Our cameras were small and light enough that the additional cost of shipping by air was more than offset by what we saved in costs by cutting out the distribution centers and reducing the amount of inventory in transit. Now we could begin building in September and still introduce worldwide before the holidays.

With this schedule, production prototypes had to be working in August. Everyone held their breath. Bad news: the production prototypes were noisy. Electronic noise is the death knell of digital cameras as it causes blurry and grainy images. Marketing prepared a contingency plan that introduced the camera after the holidays at a reduced price and no profit. Things looked bleak.

Right when I had almost given up hope, a manager from the finance department told me that if the big-zoom camera missed schedule, I would be the first one fired. Great. I countered, saying that I'd rather be fired for trying to help the camera business succeed than keep my job while everyone else lost theirs.

Paul and his team knew what was at stake. They worked around the clock throughout August, cancelling vacations, working weekends, essentially living at work. Miraculously, their commitment paid off and the noise problem was resolved just in time for production launch.

More bad news: the contract manufacturer couldn't build high enough quality cameras in production. Paul sent one of his engineers to Asia, where he spent months helping the contract manufacturer and its suppliers build cameras that met our quality requirements.

Building Consensus

Suddenly, our expected sales forecast tripled. I and others on my team traveled the world urging suppliers to ramp up production. Sony agreed to provide more four megapixel sensors, although the Sony salesman couldn't imagine why we wanted more. With sensors in hand, Fujinon held the key to our success. Lens production was a precise and slow process, as it has been for centuries. Worse, Fujinon was a subsidiary of Fujifilm, a competitor. I doubted that Fujinon would increase its lens production for us, but I knew I needed to try.

I arrived in Tokyo and met with the CEO of Fujinon. I thanked him a dozen times for designing and building a custom lens on an accelerated schedule. Then I asked for the impossible: triple production. Amazingly, Fujinon agreed to do it.

Our big-zoom camera went head-to-head against five-megapixel, 3X optical zoom cameras from Sony, Canon, and other Japanese heavy-weights and kicked butt. It was named "Camera of the Year" in a leading German camera magazine. Thanks primarily to the European sales team, the big-zoom camera earned $150 million in revenue at 13 percent profit, lifting the company's camera business well into profitability for the first time ever. Suddenly, no one was talking about shutting down the camera business. It was truly a heroic achievement.

I traveled to thank the players that made it happen: the team at the European marketing center, the contract manufacturer, and Fujinon. I asked the CEO of Fujinon why he and his team worked so hard to help us succeed when Fujinon was a subsidiary of our competitor. He said, "Your team is more fun to work with." Needless to say, that was the last time the digital camera business bought any components from Sony.

In two years, our company's digital camera revenue increased from $200 million to $450 million and the $100-million-dollar loss was turned into a respectable profit. With the scanner and camera businesses turned around, my career went ballistic. I was now a vice president and general manager; I was responsible for the scanner and digital camera businesses, which had a combined revenue of just under $1 billion.

The company had just completed a difficult merger. The CEO held an executive meeting in San Francisco at a swanky hotel. As a newly minted vice president, I joined the other vice presidents, senior vice presidents, and executive vice presidents to listen to the CEO speak about the future of the company.

After thanking everyone and describing the challenges ahead, the CEO told the audience that there was one business within the company that demonstrated how to succeed in a very competitive industry during difficult economic times: the camera business. That was unexpected—I should enjoy the success. It wouldn't last.

Building Consensus

Commercial success in the face of adversity requires the

Building Consensus

ability to build consensus among larger teams that contain people with very different, but complementary, expertise. Building consensus can bring larger teams together, improve the quality of team decisions, increase employee commitment to the success of a product, and effectively use staff's nontraditional skills and creativity. Employees become engaged and committed when they have an opportunity to define their own goals, have a say in important decisions, and create their own action plans.[1]

The big-zoom camera was successful because it was built using consensus. It was the product that the engineering department wanted to design, using a lens Fujinon wanted to build, housed in a design that the European sales force would be proud to sell.

The first step in building consensus is empowerment. Marilyn empowered me and my organization by persuading the CEO and senior executives to allow the camera business to continue.

The second step is accurately defining the problem and being flexible when faced with unexpected obstacles. The digital camera business had to quickly define and develop a profitable new product or it was going to be shut down. People who were uncomfortable with change soon realized that a flexible product development plan was necessary, given the unexpected hurdles we faced.

Third is casting a wide net for ideas. When breakthroughs are needed, it's best to ask a lot of people for their ideas. It didn't take long for Dave to propose a consumer big-zoom camera.

Fourth is accepting the issues. Criticism is difficult to hear, but critical people are often trying to help. If the criticism is brushed aside, people will lose confidence in the project and the leader. They will not believe that their thoughts and opinions are being heard or matter to the team, resulting in them being less invested in resolving the issues. Our development plan initially had a gaping weakness: design.

Fifth is asking for help. Asking for help usually works because over 90 percent of adults—group two plus group three, are willing, if not anxious, to help if the cause is just. However, group one people are not, as the newly appointed Sony executive responsible for sensor allocation demonstrated. Therefore it's important to investigate potential suppliers and partners before entering into business agreements.

Sometimes, the people who identify or are critical of an issue are best suited to solve the problem if given the opportunity and any needed support. The European marketing center had a designer with the skills required to design a sleek, user-friendly camera. And involving the European marketing center in the product development increased their commitment to sell the product.

Sixth, communicate often, regarding both accomplishments and problems. People need to know what's going on. Although it's tempting to communicate only good news, communicating problems gives others an opportunity to help.

Building Consensus

Last is making it fun. If working together is fun, it can motivate people to help who otherwise wouldn't. When the demand forecast tripled, Fujinon came to the rescue because their people enjoyed working with us, even though helping us hurt their parent company Fujifilm.

Bottom Line: Effectively building consensus can enable mission-critical projects and ultimately companies to succeed that otherwise wouldn't.

Chapter 11

Return of the Plunderers

"At my former company, this was the time of year when we'd figure out how many people we had to lay off to get our bonuses." I nearly spit out the bite of chicken I was chewing. It was mid-December, smack dab in the middle of the holidays. I recovered my composure and checked to see if Wesley, a fellow vice president, was kidding. He wasn't.

Wesley knew that Wall Street loved layoffs. Layoffs increase profit in the short term by reducing cost but keeping revenue fairly constant. In the long term, layoffs cause a company's ability to innovate or improve its processes to suffer, then their products become stale and customer satisfaction declines. The organizations are ultimately worse off. But these problems manifest three to five years down the road—smart plunderers will have cashed out by then.

As a new vice president, I joined ten other executives, including Wesley, in a newly formed business unit with a mission to grow revenue and profit. We were all working for Marilyn.

I worked with other executives to propose a potentially lucrative business opportunity that leveraged the unique strengths within multiple businesses. This was exactly the type of opportunity the business unit was formed to do. But Wesley strongly opposed my idea, making my goal of building consensus impossible. He opposed other value-creating opportunities too. He wasn't the only one.

Having been on a fast track towards the coveted corner office at his former company, Wesley campaigned tirelessly, if not subtly, for a quick promotion. He told several of us that the business unit would be far more profitable if he was the boss instead of Marilyn. He was quick to blame others, which disrupted the team dynamic. He had the same solution for every problem: layoffs. Soon, the team culture degraded into every man and woman for his or her self.

Before long, Marilyn announced that she was retiring. Unfortunately for Wesley, management wasn't impressed by his hyper-competitive style and slash-and-burn ideas. He didn't get the promotion he coveted and left the company in a bit of a huff.

Wesley should have stayed. A few months later, the company hired Mark to be its new CEO. Mark made it clear that he expected the stock price to increase a lot because he would make sure the company's profit goals were met every quarter, no matter what the cost. Because the stock was still down 85 percent from its Dotcom-era high, many employees were so happy to hear that the stock price would increase that they didn't seem to notice when Mark said that the method by which he would ensure the profit goals were met would be through workforce cost reduction. In other words, layoffs.

How did it come to this? The board of directors ran out of patience with the former CEO. Under his watch, a high-profile merger had failed to deliver its projected profit, and the new products weren't particularly successful.

What the company needed was to build ethical teams to develop new products and develop new business opportunities. Instead, they put a plunderer in charge.

My career took a U-turn shortly after Marilyn left. My new boss and I didn't see eye to eye. I was soon demoted from my vice president and general manager job and assigned to Nick, the senior vice president of operations. I was back to being a director again.

Nick told me that my experience working with Asian suppliers made me uniquely qualified to do exactly what Mark wanted: move American jobs to low-cost workers in developing countries.

In response, I suggested helping the company leverage its global partners to develop new products, as we had done in chapters 9 and 10. Nick and I had a few long talks about this, talks in which I tried to convince him that globalization's true potential lies in using diverse partners to create value for all impacted parties:

investors, employees, customers, and communities. Nick viewed globalization as simple economics: cost is reduced by replacing high-cost workers with low-cost workers. I told him that he was comparing apples to oranges, because highly-skilled American professionals that build successful businesses can't simply be replaced by inexperienced college graduates in low-cost developing countries. I explained that a competitive advantage can be gained by harnessing the skills and abilities of a global workforce to ensure the success of current businesses while also developing innovative new products and processes and building new businesses. What Nick and Mark were planning was unethical because it harmed workers. It was also disastrous for the business because it destroyed the company's ability to develop new products and processes and build new businesses.

Nick's mind was made up. He even created a catch phrase for this type of plundering, "capturing value." New products and new businesses create value, but the company wasn't doing much of that anymore. Layoffs capture value, in that people lose their jobs and the money saved is "captured" for investors and executives. Actually, layoffs destroy a company's value—effective teams are broken up, institutional knowledge is lost, and employee morale suffers.

During one meeting, Nick arranged for one of his managers to present his favorite outsourcing success story. The manager had moved product qualification testing from a design center in America to India. The manager bragged that hourly costs for testing were cut in half.

After the meeting, I called the manager and asked a few questions. I learned that the number of test hours more than doubled, which then caused the new product to miss its scheduled release. The truth behind this "success" story was that Americans lost their jobs, the cost of product development increased, and the product missed its scheduled release date, reducing the company's revenue and profit. Nick was angling to institute a group lie that he was reducing cost through outsourcing, when he was actually increasing costs.

I explained to the manager that the high level of interdependence and skill required to successfully develop new products make it difficult to move product qualification testing 8,500 miles away from the rest of product development and staff it with people that are unfamiliar with the product. The manager said he did what he was told. Nick was right about one thing—he needed help. The kicker: Mark had increased bonuses for directors to 70 percent of base salary. I saw that I could make a lot of money plundering.

Wait. Don't I have a book about plundering? Yes, the *Attila* book. I'll bet Nick and Mark would find the story of how one man dominated a vast territory by promoting the principles of death for the disloyal, lust for leadership, and courage to win at all costs. But that option wasn't for me, so I left in the first big wave of layoffs. I had saved enough money to say "no" to plunderers.

Return of the Plunderers

After I left, Mark quickly proved that he belonged in the Plunderer's Hall of Fame. Soon layoffs occurred almost every week. New businesses were shut down. New products were canceled. The research and development (R&D) department was gutted. Mark took the money R&D was investing in building a future for the company and invested it in himself. In many areas, layoffs cut the number of staff, but the workload stayed the same. Employees worked backbreaking hours; several became ill. The company spent a fortune buying back its stock, more than its entire profit, to the delight of Wall Street.[1] All the while Mark promoted group lies about his decision, saying, "We're cutting fat" and "We're positioning the company for future growth." Had he stayed, Wesley would have found a kindred spirit.

Then Mark made a fatal mistake: he stayed too long. After a few years, the company's products became stale. Quality deteriorated. The company's stock peaked and started back down. Suddenly, Mark was fired for falsifying expense reports. He was caught after a contractor sued him for sexual harassment. A quick internal investigation revealed that Mark had falsified expense statements to have the company pay for hotel rooms and dinners for the contractor. His ever-changing story was the last straw.[2] (A piece of advice: when caught, don't lie. One can often be forgiven for breaking the rules. Lying about it destroys the trust required to rebuild relationships.)

Teams vs. Plunderers

Several CEOs, also plunderers, ran to Mark's defense, and criticized the board of directors for firing him. The board of unethical directors might have overlooked Mark's expense report fraud and the sexual harassment accusations had the stock price been rising. In the end, despite his misdeeds, Mark still walked away with tens of millions of dollars.

I wonder if this was the first time Mark stole from his employer or if it was the first time he was accused of sexually harassment. Perhaps it was just the first time he had been caught.

The Pressure to Plunder

After I told Nick that I wasn't going to move American jobs to developing countries with low-cost labor, he told me that I don't have what it takes to be an executive. Fine by me.

Sooner or later, plunderers will ask their employees to plunder. Employees may be asked to ship defective products, execute unnecessary layoffs, put workers' health and safety at risk, renege on promises, illegally manipulate earnings, or side-step pollution controls. Monetary rewards and potential promotions may be used to entice employees to plunder. Mark offered large bonuses to executives who would do his dirty work and unemployment to those who wouldn't. Under a plunderer like Mark, if an employee, and particularly a manager, refused to adhere to the party line or group lie, his career is most likely over at that company. If he plunders, his career is intact.

Return of the Plunderers

I was asked to plunder. I refused, and my career ended at this company. My past efforts, my years of contribution, meant nothing.

Bottom line: Beware—sooner or later many employees will be pressured to plunder

Chapter 12

Building Ethical and Effective Organizations

A growing number of people, particularly young people, are taking a stand against organizations and individuals that plunder. With the advent of social media, news of bad actors can spread to the edges of the globe within the span of a 24-hour news cycle. Customers are becoming emboldened to use the power of their dollars, particularly the power that stems from withholding those dollars, to chastise those who plunder.

As a result, many corporate leaders recognize that their organizations need to be socially and environmentally responsible in addition to delivering a good product to customers and a return to investors. For some leaders, the challenge is to keep improving. For companies that plunder, the challenge is nothing short of recreating their companies.

To meet the increasing societal demand for ethical companies, organizations should:

Building Ethical and Effective Organizations

1. Hire good leaders;
2. Weed out plunderers;
3. Build ethical teams; and
4. Build consensus.

Hire Ethical and Effective Leaders

There are several reasons for hiring ethical and effective people into leadership positions. First and foremost, ethical and effective leaders will not plunder. Many managers are under pressure to increase revenue and profit or reduce cost. Plundering is one way to do it. Ethical and effective leaders will look for solutions that avoid plundering because their behavior is driven by internal moral principles. They may ascribe to a "do no harm" principle or other tenets of morality. But in the end, ethical and effective leaders will create value, rather than capturing it.

Second, people trust and respect ethical and effective leaders. As like attracts like, ethical and effective leaders attract people who are also ethical and effective and provide them with an opportunity to flourish. Third, hiring ethical and effective leaders encourages the vast majority of adults, who are known to behave in a way they think the boss will approve of, to behave ethically.

Ethical leaders:
1. Have integrity;
2. Are active listeners;
3. Are trustworthy;
4. Take responsibility for problems; and

5. Are willing to be approached about any topic.

Today, ethical and effective leaders are rare because plunderers are embedded throughout corporate America. But ethical leaders are more effective at creating value than plunderers; the key to an ethical leader's effectiveness is raising the performance of people around her. The below chart describes my performance as an employee under three different types of leaders.

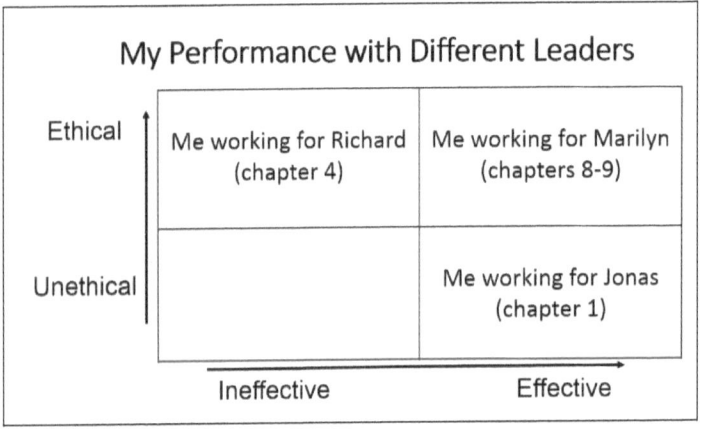

I was unethical, yet effective under Jonas' leadership. This was mainly due to the fact that I deceived Jonas into believing I embraced his medieval management style. As a reward for helping a plunderer succeed, I received a large raise and stock options. But I had no real power—was unable to protect those within my department.

Building Ethical and Effective Organizations

Under Richard, I was ethical, but ineffective. I tried and failed to protect customers from receiving defective tape libraries. At the end of the day, I was lucky to keep my job.

Working for Marilyn, my performance was both ethical and effective. I helped turn around two businesses that were given up for dead and was promoted to vice president and general manager. Just eight years earlier, I was a failing first-level manager working for Gomer. Under Marilyn's leadership, I saw others' performance improve as well—some even ended up being more successful than me.

Raising Performance

Ethical and effective leaders provide their employees with the following benefits:
1. Professional development;
2. Mentorship;
3. Experience building and interacting with ethical teams; and
4. Experience building consensus among larger teams, which include individuals that are under no obligation to help.

Many corporate leaders tell employees that their careers are their responsibility. Some consider themselves progressive because they offer free training or reimburse their employee's continued education. This is a cop out. A new or front-line employee isn't going to know what an organization needs and how to provide it. Knowing that, an ethical and effective leader will provide her employees with the skills, training, and resources needed to succeed at their job.

Four months after I began working for Marilyn, she scheduled a one-on-one meeting with me. I thought I was in trouble for criticizing the decision to build my new product only in Singapore. Instead, she told me that I had good business sense and that she appreciated hearing about problems that needed to be solved for the business to succeed. This was a relief because identifying problems had gotten me into trouble with a number of other bosses.

Marilyn then asked if I would be interested in taking on broader business responsibilities. She said I had the potential to lead a business one day as a general manager. I had never considered managing a business before this conversation—I was a manufacturing guy. But, after telling Marilyn that I was interested, she asked me to join the cross-functional business strategy team as the manufacturing representative. She had been the previous manufacturing representative, and she even volunteered to cover meetings if I was traveling. In four months, she had mapped out a route to a successful career for me. She then handed me the reins, gave me a compass and some hard tack, and sent me on my way. Being a new first-level manager, I had no idea what career options were available to me, much less any idea how to figure out how to get there.

For nearly three years, until Brett became general

manager, I was a member of the business strategy team. Marilyn also recommended me to other cross-functional teams. Through these experiences, I gained crucial knowledge about developing viable business strategies, collaborating with others, and managing a business, knowledge that I relied upon when leading the scanner and digital camera businesses. No other manager, and I worked for twenty-plus managers, supported me as Marilyn did.

Bottom line: Bosses matter.

Weed out Plunderers

Instead of weeding out employees who won't plunder, organizations should weed out the plunderers. Here's how:
1. Pay attention to actions, rather than carefully maintained images;
2. Be skeptical of ideas or reports that seem to be too good to be true;
3. Develop a plan; and
4. Take action.

The first two steps identify the group lies, in-group bias, and groupthink plunderers use to justify their unethical actions. The last two deal with it.

It's easier for those who are being directly blamed or harmed to spot group lies, in-group bias, and groupthink than it is for people who aren't. In chapter 3, I knew immediately that the cartridge operations department was being wrongly blamed for a disk drive problem. I knew because I bore the brunt of the harm, and had to work all night to set up a screen test for an issue that wouldn't be resolved until the underlying disk drive defect was fixed. In chapter 4, it took me longer to realize that women and minorities were being discriminated against because, as a white male, I didn't feel the in-group bias's harmful effects. But, eventually, I heard about it from others. After that, I could easily spot the damage this bias caused. At MiniScribe, I likely didn't see the wrongdoing that was going on because it didn't directly affect me and I traveled a lot. Even when I was told by someone who had first-hand knowledge that the company was cheating, I didn't believe it. From that experience I learned it's important to pay attention and to be skeptical.

Weeding out plunderers can be challenging because they often hold the highest positions, and they aren't going to give up their high-paying jobs without a fight. Q.T. Wiles, Richard, and Mark were CEOs. Jonas, Wesley, and Arthur were vice presidents.

Some plunderers, like Jonas and Wesley, are easy to spot. Others, like Q.T. Wiles, Richard, and Bruce, are wolves in sheep's clothing. **The key to spotting plunderers at the top is paying attention to what happens as a result of their management, not what leaders say or who enforces the policies they set.**

If plundering is happening, leaders are either directing it, encouraging it through rewards and/or punishment, or condoning it by looking the other way.

Building Ethical and Effective Organizations

If leaders don't want plundering to occur, they could stop it, just as they stop other activities that don't generate revenue and profit. If plunderers are at the top, it's time to find a new job.

To ensure that you always have the power to say "no" to plunderers, plan ahead and prepare for the worst by: (1) developing a cash reserve; (2) developing a professional network; and (3) identifying exit triggers. For the cash reserve, a good rule of thumb is that you should have saved enough to cover your expenses for three to six months. To develop a professional network, you should reach out to your peers, get to know your colleagues, and talk to other folks in your industry that hold positions that you aspire to obtain. You can then use your network to find out which employers and managers are effective, supportive, and ethical. That's how I found Marilyn, a boss with internal moral principles. Finally, exit triggers should be identified. Don't wait to be asked to plunder or to be a victim of plundering. Take action immediately.

Today, employees of plundering organizations have more options. If their employer commits a crime, whistleblower laws provide potentially large financial rewards and some protection from potential repercussions and retaliation. The first priority is to protect yourself. Don't be surprised if your manager or the human resources department dismisses your issue, or worse, decides you're at fault. The safest way to blow the whistle is after you've secured another job.

Teams vs. Plunderers

Susan Fowler ignited a firestorm when she blogged about the sexual harassment she endured while working for Uber. Six months later, Uber CEO Travis Kalanick, the most celebrated and richest startup CEO in Silicon Valley, was forced to resign. Fowler wrote her blog after finding another job. After making multiple complaints to Uber's human resources department, she decided that human resources would not protect her—so she devised a plan to protect herself.

Plunderers make tempting promises. Mark raced to the top by seducing management and boards of unethical directors with propositions like, "Let's make a lot of money. All we have to do is lay off enough people to make our quarterly profit numbers and our annual bonuses. Then we use the money saved to buy back the company's stock. It's easy." These two actions can increase a senior executive's annual compensation by hundreds of thousands of dollars and a CEO's compensation by millions. Customer satisfaction isn't required. Mark then exonerates himself and his fellow plunderers with group lies, such as, "We're positioning the company for future growth". Given the size of the windfall, plunderers and their followers can usually shut down any discussions about the long-term harm these actions inflict on the company.

Because ethical and effective leaders leverage the unique skills of the people around them, they can make the mistake of giving plunderers important responsibilities and second chances. This can be all a plunderer needs to disrupt value creation efforts and sabotage their leader—or maybe even steal her job.[1]

The best time to identify plunderers is before they reach the top. To prevent this outcome, ethical and effective leaders can use the four steps outlined above. Leaders should pay close attention to how aspiring leaders behave, particularly as members of teams. Plunderers want to enrich themselves the easy way: at other peoples' expense. They will jump at the chance to lead or be a member of a team that plunders. And they will create and embrace group lies that exonerate the themselves of wrongdoing, as Dick and Troy did in chapter 3. But they're not interested in leading or being a member of an interdependent, value creating team because they don't want to work hard only to share credit or blame with people they consider inferior.[1] If a plunderer is stuck on one of these teams, the team will not perform up to its potential. As plunderers can be very good at blaming other team members, leaders should pay close attention and be skeptical of what they hear from members of underperforming teams.

Plunderers can also be quite adept at sabotaging efforts to build consensus, as Wesley did in the last chapter. Of course, it has always been easier to destroy than to build. **Accordingly, company leaders should consider implementing a policy to only promote people with successful experience as a team leader or member of an interdependent, value-creating team to leadership positions.** The people without this experience can be divided into two groups: the larger group is comprised of people who work best alone or on straight-forward projects with independent, non-competing goals. These people can manage small single-skill-set groups but will most likely struggle if given broader responsibility. But the second group of people, those people who disrupt value creation efforts, are most likely serial plunderers and need to be managed out. This may sound extreme until one considers how much damage they can do.

Imagine how much value organizations can create if they weren't plagued by plunderers.

Assemble Ethical Teams

With ethical and effective leaders in charge and plunderers out of the picture, organizations can build ethical teams that will create value for the company, its customers, its employees, and the greater community.

Ethical teams take on audacious goals and search outside of the traditional methods of operation for innovative solutions that satisfy everyone's needs. They identify what can go wrong and develop plans that minimize risk before moving forward.

Ethical team elements include:
1. A noble mission or purpose;
2. Needed skills;
3. Interdependent team members;
4. A supportive environment; and
5. Commitment to everyone's success, rather than individual success.

Building Ethical and Effective Organizations

Once a company gains a reputation for taking on and solving social and environmental problems, ethical and effective people will want to join. These people will help advance social and environmental accomplishments, which will further improve a company's reputation, thus accelerating the cycle.

The keys to building an ethical team are (1) staffing the team with people that have needed skills and (2) creating a supportive environment in which the team can operate. Team members must be committed to each other's success, as well as their own success. The trust built from that commitment to everyone's success produces the confidence required to tackle hard problems, find common ground, and collaborate until breakthroughs are found that achieve everyone's goals, as the ethical team did in chapter 9. Without a commitment to everyone's success, the hard problems encountered along the way will create ethical dilemmas for the individual team, causing people to retreat to their narrow department goals, ultimately fragmenting the team, as happened to the teams in chapter 5, 6, and 7.

Ethical and effective leaders will create the supportive environment needed for ethical teams to thrive. Sometimes these leaders have to swap out team members or remove obstacles, such as resistance to change.

Companies can quickly fail if their success relies upon building ethical teams and they don't know how.

Three of the six tech companies I worked for no longer exist because they couldn't put together an ethical team when they needed one. Although building ethical teams may require more work on the front-end than plundering does, the results are superior, the effects are long-lasting, and employees are happier because they can act in accordance with their internal moral principles.

Build Consensus

Finding solutions to hard problems, while satisfying all stakeholders, often requires larger teams comprised of people with varied areas expertise. Along the way, you may even get help from those who are under no obligation to do so. Successfully leveraging these various skill sets first requires building consensus.

People become more engaged in, and committed to, implementing a business strategy when they have an opportunity to define their own goals, shape important decisions, and create their own action plans.[1] Consensus-building produces better results because it taps into a variety of skills, which improves the resulting decisions, and increases employee commitment to the success of the project.

The big zoom camera, described in chapter 10, would not have succeeded without the contribution of two external groups: the European marketing team and Fujinon. Both groups provided more help than I expected and far more than they had to. This is to be expected, as most people will help if asked. Sony however provided less help than expected. Sony tried to use the its sensor business as a lever to advance its camera business at the expense of our camera business, even though our camera business had been a reliable customer.

To build consensus, a leader must:
1. Empower its team members;
2. Accurately define the problem;
3. Cast a wide net for ideas;
4. Accept issues and criticism;
5. Ask for help;
6. Communicate consistently; and
7. Make it fun.

Bottom Line: Let's say "no" to plundering and "yes" to ethical teams.

Chapter 13

When Tech Companies Attack

Imagine the sinking feeling when you realize that the leading-edge tech company you partnered with is stealing your customers. That was the feeling I felt when Sony reneged on its commitment to provide us with sensors.

Sony made the best sensors, according to our engineers, based upon the tests they performed. And for years, Sony had been a reliable supplier. But soon after I joined the digital camera business, it appeared that Sony adopted a new strategy: secure customers for its sensors, make commitments to those customers, wait until it's too late for customers to switch to another sensor supplier, then renege on those commitments, and divert sensor supply to Sony's cameras in order to steal market share from its customers—especially us.

The first step in dealing with problems of this magnitude is accepting the fact that the business is in big trouble and may even be entering a death spiral. The second step is relentlessly searching for a solution that fends off the attacking tech company. This can be

When Tech Companies Attack

difficult because the attacking tech company has probably been planning its attack for months, if not years. It's times like these that companies need ethical and effective organizations to assemble ethical teams and build needed consensus. Time is of the essence.

We were able to quickly turn the tables on Sony because we accepted the fact that we had to do something immediately. Most important, we found a solution: a big-zoom camera with Sony's four megapixel sensors that customers preferred over Sony's five mega-pixel cameras. The chart shows how value in the relationship between us and Sony began as balanced, then shifted to Sony, and then back to us.[1]

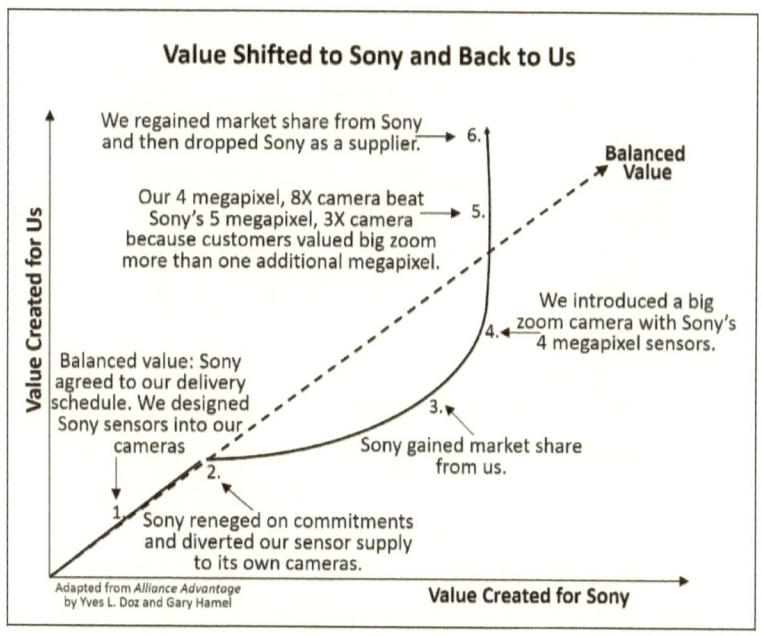

When Tech Companies Attack

Turning Competitors into Allies

Top managers in the scanner business either did not accept the fact that the business had entered a death spiral or that they needed to do something about it. Instead, they stayed the course for over two years, as market share fell from 45 percent to 18 percent and profit turned into losses.

The attack on our scanner business had been planned for years. The country of Taiwan decided it would fund Taiwanese companies to enter and dominate the scanner industry. This was part of Taiwan's larger strategy to succeed in the tech industry. New sensors with on-chip color separation had reduced the barriers to entry. Previously, manufacturers had to use high precision, tight-tolerance, beam-splitting prisms to split white light into red, green, and blue components and shine the different light components onto specific rows of photo-sensitive pixels on a sensor. Because of the new sensors and government funding, ten Taiwanese companies aggressively entered the market and targeted the market leader—us.

By the time my team was formed, there wasn't money, people, or time to design a complete new low-cost product: hardware plus software. Worse, the solution proposed by the scanner business executives—purchase entire products, add third-party software, and then slap our company's logo on them—would have failed. We were backed into a corner. We had to try

When Tech Companies Attack

something different.

With Marilyn's help, I was able to build an ethical team that successfully developed two new products on an accelerated schedule. But it was the $99 product that energized the sales force and convinced retailers to stock our products on their shelves. The key to the rapid development of the $99 product was turning the market leader or another competitor into a reliable supplier. This was risky. Had the Taiwanese companies joined forces and refused to sell us hardware, we would have failed. The market leader also could have caused us to fail by waiting until it was too late to switch suppliers and then withholding supply, as Sony did.

From the beginning of the relationship with the market leader, we acted in good faith. Our engineers created a technical interface between our software and the market leader's hardware that enabled engineers from both companies to work effectively together and achieve excellent performance and image quality. (Our engineers did the same with the supplier that provided hardware for the $199 product.) We also paid our bills promptly.

By acting ethically, trust was built that motivated the market leader to also act ethically. The market leader provided us with high-quality hardware on schedule that enabled us to sell two million units of the $99 product and regain market leadership. The now former market leader became a reliable supplier for years to come.

When Tech Companies Attack

The chart shows how the value between us and the Taiwanese competitor began with us having more value, then value shifted to the Taiwanese competitor because of its lower price, and then back to us because customers valued our software.[1]

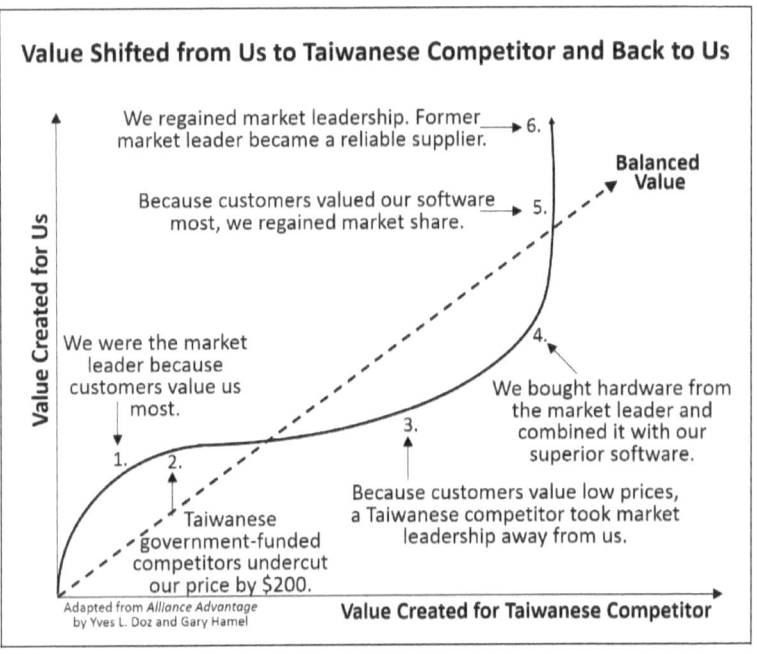

When Tech Attacks, Customer Loss Can Be Rapid

In a little over two years, government-funded Taiwanese scanner companies were able to drive our market share down from 45 percent to 18 percent and turn our profits into losses.

Rapid customer loss is a relatively new phenomenon that can occur when tech companies

When Tech Companies Attack

attack. Traditionally, attacks in non-tech industries produce much slower customer loss. For instance, 54 years were required for Japanese, German, and Korean automakers to drive General Motors' U.S. market share down from 51 percent to 17 percent.[2] Because customer loss was much slower, General Motors (GM) was able to use workforce reductions and a government bailout to remain in business. From its peak in 1979 to 2017, the number of GM U.S. employees decreased 83 percent from 618,000 to 103,000.[3,4] At times, GM has even been quite profitable, despite the fact that the company still hasn't figured out how to build vehicles with enough value to fend off its attackers.

When tech companies attack, workforce reductions can backfire because by the time the layoffs are complete and the remaining employees have learned their new jobs, too many customers have already left. Workforce reductions can also make organizations less ethical and therefore less able to find solutions needed to fend off attackers.

Most non-tech company leaders aren't prepared for the rapid loss of customers that results from an attack by tech companies. Consequently, their leaders have made the same mistake the scanner managers initially made: they don't accept the fact that their business is in big trouble and that they need to immediately and relentlessly search for a solution that fends off the attacking tech company. As a result, tech companies have rapidly stolen customers from non-tech industries that had been stable for decades, including bookstores, electronics retailers, department stores, and print newspapers. Many previously high-flying companies have already shut down, including: Circuit City, Borders, Blockbuster, Toys "R" Us, and many others.

When Tech Attacks, Everything is Legal (almost)

The tech community has learned that laws designed in another era to establish standards of business conduct can often be broken by tech companies with little or no consequence. Microsoft was a pioneer. Federal investigations into Microsoft began in 1992, after several companies accused Microsoft of illegally using its monopoly in operating systems to enter adjacent software markets, including the fast-growing spreadsheets and word processing markets. While the investigations continued, Microsoft's Word and Excel quickly surpassed former industry leaders WordPerfect and Lotus and, by 1995, had captured over 70 percent market share in their respective markets.

Then the Internet happened, and Microsoft was late to embrace it. In 1995, Netscape's Navigator became the leader in web browsers. Microsoft scrambled to catch up, but customers preferred Netscape's Navigator over Microsoft's Internet Explorer. In 1998, Netscape's Navigator was still trouncing Internet Explorer. Microsoft decided to require its PC-maker customers to install its Internet Explorer with its Windows operating system and sell it for free.[5] Any PC-maker that refused would not be allowed to buy Microsoft's operating system. In 1998, Microsoft's market share in operating systems was nearly 90%.[5]

In 1998, the U.S. Department of Justice and twenty states sued Microsoft for anti-competitive behavior. In 1999, a judge found Microsoft guilty of violating the Sherman anti-trust act. By then, Microsoft's Internet Explorer had already raced past Netscape's Navigator to become the market-leading web browser. In 2000, the same judge ordered that Microsoft be broken into two companies: one that sold operating systems and a second that sold other products.[6] Many in the tech industry rejoiced as it appeared that the legal system had finally caught up with Microsoft.

Then Microsoft appealed. In 2001, a different judge upheld the verdict but not the punishment.[6] This judge ruled that the prosecution had failed to prove that Microsoft's action that forced its PC-maker customers to tie Internet Explorer to Windows had harmed competition, even though Netscape was reeling.[6] The prosecution even failed to establish that there is a difference between software and software products, to the delight of Microsoft.[6] Consequently, the new settlement required that Microsoft merely share its applications program interface (API) with application developers. (The API in question was Microsoft's software program that communicates between Microsoft's operating system and Microsoft and non-Microsoft application programs.) Microsoft was free to continue to interfere with a Windows user's choice of web browser software products and other non-Microsoft products.[6] Nine states appealed, arguing that this slap on the wrist would not curb Microsoft's anti-competitive practices. By 2004, all nine states had lost their appeals and Internet Explorer's market share had reached 95 percent.[6,7] In 2002, Netscape was sold to AOL.

The tech industry and particularly tech startups learned a valuable lesson: lawmakers, regulators, enforcements agents, and judges don't understand technology well enough to write effective laws or regulations, to fully grasp the ramifications of tech plunderers' actions, or to adjudicate fairly. Consequently, by the time the wheels of justice turn, if they turn at all, tech companies can steal enough customers to conquer a market and leave the competition for dead. As a result, lawbreaking has become ingrained in Silicon Valley, as Amazon, Uber, Theranos, Zenefits, and others have demonstrated.[8,9]

Beware of Tech Partners

Traditionally, companies have pursued win-win relationships with other companies. But tech companies often enter relationships with the goal of stealing customers from their business partners.

Here's an example: In 2003, Amazon began selling toys from other retailers on its website, in violation of its contract with Toys "R" Us, which stipulated that Amazon could only sell Toys "R" Us toys. Toys "R" Us sued and won, but by the time Amazon had exhausted its appeals and paid Toys "R" Us $51 million, six years had passed, Amazon was the king of online toy sales, and Toys "R" Us was nearly dead.[10] Amazon wasn't the only cause of Toys "R" Us' demise. Toys "R" Us made other ill-fated decisions, such as borrowing billions to take the company private. Still, a paltry $51 million dollar fine six years after violating its contract was a lucrative investment for Amazon.[10]

Often lawbreaking isn't required to steal customers. Merely unethical behavior will suffice, as Amazon has demonstrated with book publishers. In 2007, Amazon priced brand-new, Kindle e-books from best-selling authors at $9.99, roughly a five-dollar loss per e-book, when traditional bookstores priced the same hardcover book at $29.99 — this after book publishers prepared e-books for Amazon at Amazon's insistence.[8] Amazon sent a loud-and-clear message: Amazon has the willpower and financial backing to lose a lot of money in order to force traditional bookstores out of business and command sufficient market share to dictate terms to book publishers. After realizing he'd been duped, one publishing executive said, "It was just one more nail in the coffin that no one realized was being closed over (us), even while we were engaged every single day in a conversation about it."[8] From 2004 to 2011, the number of bookstores in America fell from 25 percent 38,539 to 29,067.[11]

Because of the speed with which tech companies can steal customers, it's more important than ever to thoroughly investigate the business practices of potential tech partners.

New Rules

In today's technology-driven world, no company is safe from an attack by a tech company. These tech company attacks are different from traditional competition. Rapid customer loss is the new normal, and the legal system favors the attackers.

Bottom Line: When tech companies attack, ethical and effective organizations are needed to assemble ethical teams and build the consensus required to find solutions that fend off attackers before it's too late.

Acknowledgements

This book would not exist without the help of a few extraordinary people. Stephanie Minnock, my editor and niece, brought the stories alive. Chris Ray and Paul Beiser suffered through early drafts and shaped the content.

I'd also like to thank all the people who took a chance on me: the managers at eight different companies that hired me, and Colorado State University for letting me teach. I'd especially like to thank my business colleagues that found solutions that satisfied everyone's needs.

Finally, my beloved wife's unwavering support inspired me to tell my story.

Notes and References

Introduction:
1. Chouinard, Yvon, and Vincent Stanley. *The Responsible Company*. Patagonia Books, 2012.
2. Christensen, Clayton. *The Innovator's Dilemma: When New Technologies Cause Great Firms to Fail*. Harvard Business Review Press, 2016.

Chapter 1:
1. Barr, Robert. *MiniScribe Corporation: Case Study on Financial on Financial Statement Fraud*. Case Study, 2012.
2. United States v. Quentin T. Wiles, et al., 102 F.3d 1043 (10th Cir. 1996) (U.S. v. Wiles).
3. "Company Doctor." *INC.*, 1 February 1998, www.inc.com/magazine/19880201/7561.html. Accessed July 30, 2018.
4. Apodaca, Patrice. "Wiles Convicted of Fraud in MiniScribe Case." *LA Times*, 9 August 1994, articles.latimes.com/1994-08-09/business/fi-25289_1_disk-drive. Accessed July 30, 2018.
5. Soltes, Eugene. *Why They Do It: Inside the Mind of the White Collar Criminal*. PublicAffairs, 2016. Studies include: pharmaceutical salesmen (2005); accounting firm partners (1992); corporate board members (2000); CEOs are added to board members because boards include many CEOs, CFOs (2002); middle managers at manufacturing firms (1993); navy enlisted men (1982).

Notes and References

6. Trevino, Linda, and Katherine Nelson. *Managing Business Ethics: Straight Talk About How To Do It Right*. John Wiley and Sons, 2017.
7. Woodward, Bob. "Gordon Liddy Spills His Guts." *The Washington Post*, 18 May 1980, www.washingtonpost.com/archive/entertainment/books/1980/05/18/gordon-liddy-spills-his-guts/aeb77942-67e2-4c39-b249-c5628100ac1a/?utm_term=.e38afecdc8e2. Accessed July 30, 2018.

Chapter 2:

1. Roberts, Wess. *Leadership Secrets of Attila the Hun*. Warner Books, 1989.
2. Kellerman, Barbara. *Bad Leadership: What It Is, How It Happens, Why It Matters*. Harvard Business School Press, 2004.

Chapter 3:

1. Becker, Christian. *Business Ethics, Methods, and Application*. Unpublished Manuscript, 2015.
2. Walters, Joannna. "Sackler Family Members Face Mass Litigation and Criminal Investigations Over Opioids Crisis", The Guardian, November 19, 2018, www.theguardian.com/us-news/2018/nov/19/sackler-family-members-face-mass-litigation-criminal-investigations-over-opioids-crisis. Accessed November 24, 2018
3. Keefe, Patrick Radden. "The family that Built an Empire of Pain" New Yorker Magazine, October 30, 2017
4. Team Trace. "An American Crisis: 18 Facts About Gun Violence — and 6 Promising Ways to Reduce the Suffering," *The Trace*, 23 March 2018, www.thetrace.org/features/gun-violence-facts-and-solutions/. Accessed July 30, 2018.

Notes and References

5. Kevin Trenberth, US National Center for Atmospheric Research in Boulder
6. Martin, Richard. "How Fossil Fuel Executives Fooled Themselves on Climate change." MIT Technology review, November 9, 2015
7. "Who's to Blame: 12 Politicians and Execs Blocking Progress on Climate Change" Rolling Stone magazine, February 3, 2011
8. Ball, Jeffrey. "Shell Faces 'Lower Forever', Fortune magazine, February, 2018

Chapter 4:

1. Thompson, Leigh. *Making The Team: A Guide for Managers*. Pearson, 2014.
2. Hunt, Vivian, Dennis Layton, and Sara Prince. *Diversity Matters*. McKinsey & Company, 2015.

Chapter 5:

1. Trevino, Linda, and Katherine Nelson. *Managing Business Ethics: Straight Talk About How To Do It Right*. John Wiley and Sons, 2017.
2. Kohn, Stephen Martin. *The Whistleblower's Handbook: A Step-by-Step Guide to Doing What's Right and Protecting Yourself.* Lyons Press, 2011
3. Bowen, Richard. *Business Ethics Lessons Learned: A Citigroup Whistleblowers' Perspective*. GCI Publishing, 2017.

Chapter 8:

1. Marshall, George. *Don't Even Think About It: Why Our Brains Are Wired to Ignore Climate Change*. Bloomsbury Publishing, 2014.
2. Thompson, Leigh. *Making The Team: A Guide for Managers*. Pearson, 2014.

Notes and References

Chapter 9:
1. "Glass Cliff." *Investopedia*, www.investopedia.com/terms/g/glass-cliff.asp. Accessed July 30, 2018.
2. See Thompson, Leigh. *Making The Team: A Guide for Managers*. Pearson, 2014.

Chapter 10:
1. Hefte, Rachel. "How can we benefit from consensus decision-making?" *University of Minnesota*, www.extension.umn.edu/community/civic-engagement/tip-sheets/consensus-decision-making/. Accessed July 30, 2018.

Chapter 11:
1. Reich, Robert. *Saving Capitalism: For the Many, Not the Few*. Penguin Random House, 2015.
2. Lashinsky, Adam, and Doris Burke. "What Really Happened Between HP ex-CEO Mark Hurd and Jodie Foster?" *Fortune Magazine*, 5 November 2010, fortune.com/2010/11/05/what-really-happened-between-hp-ex-ceo-mark-hurd-and-jodie-fisher/. Accessed July 30, 2018.
3. Stone, Brad. *The Everything Store: Jeff Bezos and the Age of Amazon*, Back Bay Books, 2013
4. Griswold, Alison. "A dot-com era deal with Amazon marked the beginning of the end for Toys R Us", Quartz, September 18, 2017, URL: https://qz.com/1080389/a-dot-com-era-deal-with-amazon-marked-the-beginning-of-the-end-for-toys-r-us/
5. Hansell, Saul. "Toys 'R' Us Sues Amazon.com Over Exclusive Sales Agreement", New York Times, May 25, 2004

Chapter 12:
1. Babiak, Paul, and Robert Hare. *Snakes in Suits: When Psychopaths go to Work*. Harper Collins, 2006.

Notes and References

Chapter 13:
1. Doz, Yves. Hamel, Gary. Alliance Advantage: The Art of Creating Value through Partnering, Harvard Business School Books, 1998
2. "Top Vehicle Manufacturers in the US Market, 1961-2016", Knoema, Updated Wednesday, April 18, 2018, URL: https://knoema.com/infographics/floslle/top-vehicle-manufacturers-in-the-us-market- Bank, David.
3. "A brief history of General Motors Corp.", MLive Media Group, Updated Sep 14, 2008, URL: https://www.mlive.com/business/index.ssf/2008/09/a_brief_history_of_general_mot.html, Accessed December 21, 2018
4. "Number of U.S. General Motors employees from FY 2014 to FY 2016 by type (1,000s), Statistica, URL: https://www.statista.com/statistics/741381/employees-of-general-motors-by-in-us/, Accessed December 21, 2018
5. *Breaking Windows: How Bill Gates Fumbled the Future of Microsoft*, The Free Press, A Division of Simon and Schuster, Inc. 2001
6. Chin, Andrew. "Decoding Microsoft: A First Principles Approach" Wake Forest Law Review, 2005
7. Bright, Peter. "The End of an Era: Internet Explorer Drops Below 50 Percent of Web Usage", Wired, November 2, 2011, URL: https://www.wired.com/2011/11/the-end-of-an-era-internet-explorer-drops-below-50-percent-of-web-usage/, Accessed December 17, 2018.
8. Stone, Brad. *The Everything Store: Jeff Bezos and the Age of Amazon*, Back Bay Books, 2013
9. Griffith. Erin. "The Ugly Unethical Underside of Silicon Valley" Fortune, January 1, 2017
10. Griswold, Alison. "A dot-com era deal with Amazon marked the beginning of the end for Toys R Us", Quartz, September 18, 2017, URL: https://qz.com/1080389/a-dot-com-era-deal-with-amazon-marked-the-beginning-of-the-end-for-toys-r-us/

Notes and References

11. "Number of Bookstores in the United States", Statistica, URL: https://www.statista.com/statistics/249027/number-of-bookstores-in-the-us/. Accessed December 23, 2018

About the Author

Ed Minnock has worked for eight companies, including six tech companies, three of which were rough-and-tumble startups. Ed also led two turnarounds at Hewlett-Packard (HP).

Ed has over twenty-five years of management experience, including vice president and general manager at HP, where he was responsible for two businesses with combined revenue of nearly one billion dollars.

As a consultant, Ed has helped several companies improve product development and team problem solving including: Intel, Texas Instruments, Bombardier Aerospace, Kongsberg Automotive (Sweden, Norway), and Fisher and Paykel (New Zealand), among many others.

Ed earned a Master of Business Administration degree from Colorado State University and a Bachelor of Science degree in Operations Research / Industrial Engineering from Cornell University.

Ed teaches courses and guest lectures at Colorado State University and mentors startups.

Ed and his family live in Fort Collins, Colorado.

www.ingramcontent.com/pod-product-compliance
Lightning Source LLC
Chambersburg PA
CBHW031048180526
45163CB00002BA/731